# The Body of Christ...

*Clare T. Pelkey, CSJ*

# The Body of Christ...
## A Guide for Eucharistic Ministers

Clare T. Pelkey, CSJ

**AVE MARIA PRESS**
NOTRE DAME, INDIANA 46556

About the author:

**Clare Pelkey, CSJ,** has 12 years of experience as a eucharistic minister and spent nine years as Pastoral Care Director in a large suburban parish. In that time she coordinated a program for eucharistic ministers and worked with people of all ages in a variety of ministries. She has published articles in *Eucharistic Minister* and *Parish Family Digest* and she is currently engaged in writing and other creative endeavors.

She holds a bachelor of science degree in music, a master of arts degree in religion and liberal studies and has studied Clinical Pastoral Education at Central Islip Psychiatric Center on Long Island, New York.

*Permissions:*

Excerpts from THE JERUSALEM BIBLE, copyright © 1966 by Darton, Longman & Todd, Ltd. and Doubleday & Company Inc. Used by permission of the publisher.

Mary's Canticle and Psalm 23 from the *New American Bible* copyright 1970. Confraternity of Christian Doctrine, Inc. Used with permission.

---

© 1988 by Clare T. Pelkey, CSJ

All rights reserved. No part of this publication may be reproduced, stored in a retrieval system, or transmitted, in any form or by any means, electronic, mechanical, photocopying, recording, or otherwise, without the written permission of the publisher, Ave Maria Press, Notre Dame, Indiana 46556.

Library of Congress Catalog Card Number: 87-72416

International Standard Book Number: 0-87793-371-5

Printed and bound in the United States of America.

*Dedication*

To Jean, Kate, Bill and Marie

*Acknowledgments*

Father James Kane of the Albany Diocese for most of the guidelines for ministry in church and to the homebound as they appear in Chapter 4.

Sisters Mary Costello and Jean Roche of the Sisters of Mercy of the Albany Diocese for their ideas on giftedness in Chapter 1.

Jack and Sue Sweeney for instructions on and use of their computer.

The eucharistic ministers and homebound parishioners of St. Helen's Parish whose lives are a continual witness of love for their Eucharistic Lord and for one another.

# Table of Contents

Preface .................................... 8

Introduction ............................... 11

1 Eucharistic Life ......................... 14
   "I Am the Bread of Life"

2 Prayer ................................... 35
   "Take and Eat"

3 Pastoral Presence and Skills ............. 57
   "Only Say the Word
   and I Shall Be Healed"

4 Practical Guidelines ..................... 91
   "Do This in Memory of Me"

Appendix I
   Scriptural Readings
   on Eucharist and Healing ............. 127

Appendix II
   Prayers for Those Who Minister ....... 130

Suggested Readings and Tapes ............. 140

# Preface

As I reflect on my years as a eucharistic minister, many faces come before my mind's eye. There are people of all ages who not only ministered with me or received my ministry, but who also ministered to me by the witness of their lives — and their deaths in more instances than my heart wants to remember:

**Peg** — a diabetic for 60 years, who called herself "God's feather." Every day found her going out in service to anyone in need, "wherever the Holy Spirit leads me." The source of her strength? The Eucharist.

**Ma** — who welcomed the eucharistic ministers several times each week as she was dying of cancer. I had the privilege of bringing her the Eucharist as Viaticum, unsuccessfully trying to keep back the tears as her daughter and I prayed the 23rd psalm.

**Kathy** — Ma's 13-year-old granddaughter who, although a Down Syndrome child, never failed to ask me to pray with her during her hospitalization and treatment for leukemia. She joined her "Ma" less than two years later.

**Lloyd** — a tall, spare gentleman whose devotion to the Eucharist brought him to daily Mass even when he was well into his 80s. For as long as he was able, he brought candy each week to a local nursing home. He also brought love. Was not his presence there a eucharistic one?

**Mary Anne** — a shy mother in her early 30s, whose serious heart condition kept her homebound. After a year of receiving the Eucharist at home and feeling the support of a loving community of ministers, she was well enough to join them at Mass once again.

**Jim and Anne** — two senior citizen eucharistic ministers whose greatest joy was their finding one more way of serving others . . . together. Jim attended daily Mass, while Anne joked about being lazy and needing her sleep. What very few realized was that Anne was terminally ill. They were the first eucharistic ministers in their parish called — within six months of each other — to the heavenly banquet.

All eucharistic ministers have their own list of people to remember, people who have touched them, inspired them and taught them about love, faith, suffering and hope from the book and bread of their own lives. May this book provide present and future eucharistic ministers with the inspiration and desire to meet the Eucharistic Christ in the people they serve.

# Introduction

Ever since the bishops as pastors of the church initiated the ministry of the Eucharist by the laity, thousands of Catholics all over the world have responded to the call of God to participate. Their love for the Eucharist and for the people of God is evident in their response.

No matter how often one ponders this mystery and gift, no matter how many insights or inspirations are received, there is no end to the heights and depths that can be explored by those who experience a hunger and thirst for God's presence in the Eucharist. For some, participation in daily or Sunday liturgy is the source of their spiritual life and strength. For others, meditating on the eucharistic passages in scripture provides endless hours of spiritual sustenance. For all, the Eucharist seems eventually to become part of the very fiber of their being. They humbly seek to imitate their Lord in sharing their lives with others, and gradually come to realize that they are the disciples of Christ in today's world.

Yet, as can so often happen, no matter how important this ministry is and how dear to one's heart, it can become routine. There is a need to renew one's dedication periodically and to continue to develop the close relationship with God that the call to eucharistic ministry requires.

The chapters that follow are an attempt to provide the spiritual framework and nourishment for such a renewal, as well as practical ideas for preparing people for ministry. In discovering and developing spiritual qualities, gifts and pastoral skills, each minister becomes better able to be a disciple and witness of the Eucharistic Christ.

Chapter 1 traces a brief history of the Eucharist from the Last Supper to the present time. It then lays the foundation for a lived spirituality as it presents the life context wherein one can experience the Eucharistic Christ. In highlighting the themes of vocation and giftedness, it points out how each minister with his or her spiritual gift is the means through which the presence of Christ permeates the ministry.

The eucharistic meal contributes to our becoming what we eat: Christ himself. To further this growth in faith, the prayer life of the minister needs to be nurtured. Chapter 2 offers an overview of various prayer forms. Ministers who feel drawn to pray in a new way are encouraged to learn to do so as an ongoing way of encountering Christ and discerning God's presence in their lives both as individuals and as members of their parish, civic and global communities.

Just as the Eucharist is a source of healing, eucharistic ministers are called to be healing presences in the world, especially for those to whom they minister. Chapter 3 offers suggestions for developing some skills for facilitating healing through pastoral presence. Some needs of the minister are also recognized and addressed.

The final chapter presents practical guidelines for a parish or an individual minister to follow in developing and continuing the ministry to their brothers and sisters in church, at home, in the hospital, or in a nursing home.

The appendices list scriptural readings on Eucharist and healing. They also include prayers that might be appropriate in various circumstances encountered in the ministry of the Eucharist. A list of suggested readings relevant to each chapter as well as titles of music and spoken tapes, concludes the resource material.

*"I Am the Bread of Life"*

# 1
# Eucharistic Life

A eucharistic minister, bringing communion to patients in a local hospital, enters the room of an elderly woman she has never met. She introduces herself to the son and daughter who are with their mother and explains the purpose of her visit.

"She doesn't know what's going on any more," the son remarks sadly. "It won't mean anything to her."

The daughter, however, believes differently. "Mother was a frequent communicant in recent years. Perhaps if she sees the host . . . "

The eucharistic minister offers a brief prayer, then holds the host for the woman to see. Immediately the woman's face lights up in recognition. The minister has no doubt that the woman knows her Lord, and gives her the Eucharist. "They recognized him in the breaking of the bread" (Lk 24:35).

In another instance a young mother requests that ministers bring the Eucharist to her during the last stages of a terminal illness. Two or three times each week, one or more ministers go directly from daily Mass to the young woman's home where they share the Eucharist with her and pray for healing. Gradually the fear she is experiencing in the face of death and the impending separation from her family is replaced with peace, the healing peace of the Eucharistic Christ, which remains with her until her death.

Occurrences similar to these are taking place throughout the world today as the presence of Christ is shared with his body the church by members of the laity. No longer is the Eucharist considered to be in the sole possession of the clergy as it was for several centuries prior to Vatican Council II. Instead the church now calls upon all her people to return to the spirit of the early Christian followers of Jesus, to share more fully in the Liturgy of Word and Eucharist, and to bring the Eucharistic Christ to those unable to be present with the community for its public act of worship.

## Celebrating Eucharist Through History

It was during his last earthly supper, while

celebrating the Jewish Passover meal and offering thanksgiving to God for delivering his people from slavery under the Egyptians, that Jesus chose to give us the gift of himself in the form of food and drink, bread and wine: the Eucharist. (The word "Eucharist" comes from the Greek *eucharistia* meaning thanksgiving. It is Jesus himself who is the great act of thanksgiving offered to the Father.) The next day he would sacrifice his life on a cross, effectively delivering God's people from the slavery of sin.

After the resurrection and ascension of Jesus, his followers continued to go to the temple on Friday evening to celebrate the Jewish Sabbath. They would celebrate the Eucharist immediately afterward. Gathering as a community and reclining around a table, they would recall the sacrifice of Jesus on the cross, talk about his life, bless the bread and cup of wine as Jesus had done, and share it with one another.

As the number of Jews who believed in Jesus grew, the eucharistic celebration was held in a larger meeting place and the one who presided stood at a table. The others present also stood around him, thus signifying the resurrection of Jesus.

Around the middle of the first century A.D., when the believers had been expelled from the synagogue, they began to use scripture readings as part of the eucharistic celebration which now took place on the first day of the week, the day of the Lord's resurrection.

After a time of persecution, freedom of worship was granted under Constantine in the fourth century. The fifth and sixth centuries saw churches being built to accommodate the increasing number of Christians. Singing, processions and prayers of petition were added to the eucharistic celebration. The people received the consecrated bread in their hands and brought small portions home to those unable to attend.

Over the next 300 to 500 years, the church tried to combat various heresies that denied the divinity of Christ by placing increasing emphasis on his divinity. The Eucharist, which had been reserved in the sacristy for the sick, now began to be reserved in the church. The sacredness of the sacrament itself was continually stressed in contrast to the unworthiness of those who received it. The clergy came to be an elite class who possessed special powers for bringing God closer to his people. Latin, which had been the language of the Mass since the third century, was no longer the common language of the people. Since the majority of people had little opportunity for education, an unknown language only served to further emphasize the distance between God and themselves.

By the 13th century, the people were mere observers of a kind of sacred play. The clergy read the scriptures and all the other parts of the Mass. The people seldom received communion, and when they did, they knelt at an altar rail that further separated them from the sacred action. Only unleavened white bread was used and now was placed in the mouth of the communicant. The cup was no longer shared with the people.

Finally, in the 16th century, there was a concerted effort to reform the Mass. The Council of Trent, and later Pius X, promoted frequent communion, but until Vatican Council II there was no major change in the liturgy.

With the decrees of Vatican Council II, we witnessed another turning point in the historical awareness of the meaning of Eucharist. The council called the liturgy the central act of Christian worship, "the summit toward which the activity of the Church is directed . . . [and] the fountain from which all her power flows" (*Constitution on the Sacred Liturgy*, par. 10). Today, at every moment of time, the Eucharist is being celebrated, drawing humanity into union with God while simultaneously inundating human life with God's presence. The liturgy is considered "the action of Christ the priest and of His Body the Church" (*Constitution on the Sacred Liturgy*, par. 7) toward building up those in the church into the Lord's temple (cf. Eph 2:21-22). The Eucharist is a meal, a celebration shared by a family, not of blood ties but of believers. At the eucharistic meal we remember the sacrifice of Christ's life for his people and renew his presence among us. The word of scripture and the bread and wine of his body and blood continue to be his presence and our spiritual sustenance as we live out our daily lives. No longer mere observers, we are invited and encouraged to participate all during the liturgy: in singing, in silence, in listening to or proclaiming God's word, in action as servers, ushers, readers, music ministers and ministers of the Eucharist.

The liturgy is also meant to "fortify the faithful in their capacity to preach Christ through their lives" (*Constitution on the Sacred Liturgy*, par. 2). On the parish level in particular, people are striving to make their local church a place of community and of outreach to the poor and suffering members, not only of their own church, but wherever there are needs in the civic, national or global communities as well. In returning to the spirit of the early Christian community, we are relearning what it means to be eucharistic followers of Christ today. We realize we must extend ourselves in service to one another in our daily lives: to family, friends, neighbors, co-workers, yes, even to our enemies. Eucharistic ministry is one form of service, of sharing Christ with others.

## Vocation of the Minister

Men and women from all walks of life have responded to the church's invitation to serve. Just what is it that inspires people to become eucharistic ministers? Who can fully explain the source of this call and desire to serve, unless it is seen as a gift of faith given to those whom God has chosen to receive it? While each one may attempt to give his or her own reason, the role of eucharistic minister can truly be considered a vocation, a call to be the eucharistic Christ, as well as to bring his sacramental presence to others. We are to *be* the presence of Jesus just as much as, though in a way that is different from, the eucharistic meal he left us as a way of remembering him. Ultimately we must acknowledge that this call is a mystery just as every Christian vocation is a mystery, whether it is a call to marriage or the single state, the vowed religious life or the priesthood.

Several times in scripture, Jesus says that he was *sent* into the world, not that he chose to come. Neither did any one of us choose birth and life; rather, they were given to each person. Through baptism and their life of faith, eucharistic ministers are sent to give of themselves in service even as Jesus did for those whose lives were destined to come into contact with his. Just as Jesus came to show all people the love and fidelity of the Father, eucharistic ministers also faithfully live their lives in such a way as to witness to the holiness and faithfulness of God. "To be a witness does not consist in engaging in propaganda, nor even in stirring people up, . . . but in being a living mystery. It means to live in such a way that one's life would not make sense if God did not exist" (Cardinal Suhard).

As eucharistic ministers we bring the mystery of who we are to our ministry. Since most of us live what we would call "ordinary" lives, how can it be that we are in reality a living mystery? Perhaps we need to look more deeply with the eyes of faith to see how God permeates our lives with the life of Christ and thereby pours out his blessings on us and through us each day. We need to humbly recognize and celebrate our humanity and our uniqueness, and recognize daily human life as the place of God's presence since Jesus himself chose to be part of it. Because he told us he would be with us always, even till the end of time (Mt 28:20), we are all challenged to discover this spiritual reality in the 20th century.

## The Bread of Life

In one of our hymns we sing of "Christ, the bread from heav'n, broken in the sacrament of life." Most likely the words "sacrament of life" are meant to refer directly to Jesus in the eucharistic bread and wine. As our understanding of Eucharist has grown since Vatican Council II and we've gained new insights regarding God's presence in our world, we might reverently reinterpret the phrase. Life is the bread given to us each day for growth in holiness. It is life itself that is a sacrament, the place where we experience God's presence, and it is Jesus who has made human life holy by choosing to participate in every facet of it. As a human being, he shared life with us, becoming a baby, child, son, student, friend, teacher, healer, care-giver, one who served, a member of the laity in his day. Before his public life, we assume he had an occupation, probably as a carpenter. We read that he experienced joy at the wedding of Cana, when people demonstrated their faith in him, in the times he spent with friends. We know that he spent time in solitude and prayer.

He lived his love for us by permitting himself to experience the temptations in the desert, temptations we also know only too well: for power, wealth, fame. With God's help he overcame them. He knew physical weariness, lack of understanding, especially from the religious leaders of the day, and from his friends. He knew what it was like to lose a dear friend through death. Worst of all, he was betrayed and deserted by those he had come to love and trust during his three years of public life.

Jesus chose to undergo death and all the events that led up to it: physical torture and pain, the loss of a sense of his Father's presence, the final experience of letting go of this life.

He left us with a hope for new life because of his resurrection, as related in the appearances to Mary Magdalen, to the disciples on the way to Emmaus, to the apostles in the upper room, and again on the shore of the lake when he prepared breakfast for them.

Before his death he told his apostles he would be with them till the end of the world. Yet, paradoxically, he also said, "If I do not go, the Paraclete cannot come, but if I go I will send the Paraclete to you." Through the mysterious event of Pentecost they witnessed the coming of the Spirit of love. This Spirit transformed Jesus' first followers: "You together are Christ's body" (1 Cor 12:27).

Today this same Spirit is forming and transforming us. We are the body of Christ, his people. We can look at our ordinary lives in an entirely new way: as his presence and life in us. It is Jesus who lives, rejoices, suffers, dies and receives new life in his people throughout the world each moment of each day. This, too, is a mystery.

- Christ is alive today in children:
    - in their appreciation of the new wonders of their world,
    - in their obedience to their parents and teachers,
    - in their total involvement in play or studies,
    - in their struggle to find their place in society,
    - as (young or old) they honor their parents.

- Christ lives in spouses and parents:
    - who work at making a viable marriage,
    - who celebrate the successes of one another,
    - who rejoice at the birth of their children,
    - who struggle against mounting social pressures in order to instill Christian morals and values in their children,

## Eucharistic Life 25

- who know the joy of accomplishment as their children mature,
- who work hard to provide the necessities of food, clothing, shelter and health care,
- who know when to let go of their children.

• Christ lives in those who are determined to be honest, just and compassionate in their public and private lives:

- those who consciously choose to live more simply so that others may have a share in the necessities of life,
- those who volunteer their time and talents to assist humanitarian causes,
- those who appreciate and contribute their gifts to the arts,
- those who, with innumerable and unnoticed acts of kindness, make the world a better place in which to live,
- those who untiringly work for peace in the world.

• Christ is present in each person in the world, living out his passion in and through:

- all those who suffer from hunger and/or abuse,

— the elderly, the dying, the mentally and physically handicapped,

— those who care for an ill spouse or aged parents,

— those who have known the deep pain caused by a broken relationship or the death of a loved one,

— those who are homeless because of war, persecution or poverty,

— those who experience loss of any kind: employment, health, home, their own youth,

— those who are economically, spiritually or emotionally poor.

- The resurrection of Christ is experienced in the life of those who find joy in:

  — the birth of a child,

  — the exciting potential of new beginnings—a new job, a new state in life, a new relationship,

  — attaining a goal, reaching a milestone,

  — overcoming addictions,

  — reaching a new level of faith/prayer,

  — appreciation of the beauties of nature and art.

If you recognize yourself or others in some or most of these experiences, you have recognized Christ.

The Eucharistic Christ continues to draw his community together around his table: the doubters, the handicapped, the rich, the poor, the ordinary person, to celebrate and make holy, not only his death, but any and all the events of his life . . . *and our own.*

One eucharistic minister related how she experienced this holiness of all life as a revelation. She was responding to a suggestion in a prayer exercise to recall a recent experience of being hurt, and then to imagine herself standing before the crucified Christ:

"My spontaneous reaction was: 'Now I'm supposed to feel small and guilty for being upset about such a small hurt when I see the immense pain Christ suffered.' But then I was determined to try to enter into the prayer with no preconceived ideas about the outcome. After only a short time, it suddenly was revealed to me that even my small suffering was somehow a share in Christ's suffering, that it was he who was suffering in me now! The insight has stayed with me and has overflowed into other aspects of my life. If Christ suffers in me today, he must also rejoice in me, hope in me. . . . " Only through faith is it possible to see and to live this way.

With this awareness of Christ living in us, we as ministers can:

— overcome our fear of pain in order to be with those who are suffering a loss,

— refuse to feel sorry for ourselves and reach out to help others feel less lonely,

— allow others to give to us,

— rejoice with those who rejoice and weep with those who weep,

— challenge others to put their trust in God and not in the things of this world,

— dare to tell others of our love, admiration and gratitude for all they have done for us,

— declare with Jesus that "The Spirit of the Lord is upon me."

## Giftedness

A constant source of amazement in the universe is the realization that of all the creatures that exist — or have ever existed — no two are alike. We gaze at the stars and are in awe at the vastness and variety in space. We peer through a microscope and marvel at tiny unseen worlds within worlds. Turning to the realm of the human we become even more astounded when we realize that twins, triplets, or others born of multiple births have individual physical and personality traits that distinguish them from one another. The creative life principle of God that flows through each person is truly infinitely varied.

As a result of this new, or rediscovered awareness, how do we see ourselves and how do we respond to the questions that may arise as a result?

What is my role in this world?

What can I offer to the world and the times in which I live?

How can I recognize and develop my unique gift and share it with those whose lives touch my own so that the world may be a better place for my having lived in it?

It is believed that when we are called by the Lord, we are called to the fullness of our specific and unique potential. This call is not just to exercise the more general or obvious gifts, such as time, energy and activity, but to an interior gift of the Spirit. When people do not delve deeply enough into their inner selves to discover their specific gifts, they suffer pain, the pain of a deep sense of frustration whose source they may not be able to identify. In a person who has not discovered, recognized or exercised his or her personal gift, there is a real danger of a lack of self-esteem. Such a lack can lead to a loss of a sense of call and mission. A person may then devalue self and seek unconsciously to dull the resulting pain through apathy, overwork, overactivity, or other distracting substitutes meant to fill the void. It is also possible to confuse education, training, success or achievement with the notion of gift. People then identify their self-worth with the type of work they do, the degrees they have earned (or not earned), or with their position or status in the community.

When the church is true to its nature, it places emphasis on its identity as the people of God and the body of Christ. This people, already having received the gift of the Spirit, has a whole variety of gifts since each of its members is personally gifted. Everyone has a particular gift from God, "one with a gift for one thing and another with a gift for the opposite" (1 Cor 7:7). Each person called to that body has received his or her specialty from "the Spirit who distributes different gifts to different people just as he chooses" (1 Cor 12:11). It would seem from scripture that these gifts are expressed in diverse ways and in varying circumstances and do not need to be "trained or taught" but rather to be discovered, gratefully recognized and exercised for the building of the body. "You do not need anyone to teach you; the anointing he gave teaches you everything" (1 Jn 2:27).

Scripture gives us the following insights regarding persons, gifts and service:

— Each person has been given at least one gift (1 Cor 7:7) chosen by the Spirit for him or her to use to build the community (body), which we are calling service or ministry (1 Cor 14:12);

— each one's gift must be discovered and surfaced — the kingdom of God is within — through careful listening to one's own inner self (Eph 3:16-19);

— such discovery is made in a community of encouraging and affirming persons each with his or her own gift (1 Cor 12:7);

— so that each member may be recognized as "good news," contributing to making all things new (Rv 21:5).

Thus the Christian community might be described as a gift-bearing group, responsible for evoking to consciousness the gifts in one another and affirming and celebrating such gifts with joy.

## *Discerning One's Giftedness*

The scriptures name the gifts of the Spirit: wisdom, understanding, counsel, knowledge, piety, fortitude and fear of the Lord. But there are many other gifts that flow from these and they are not spelled out specifically in the scriptures. There are as many gifts as there are people. And the basis of all the gifts is love (1 Cor 8:1).

Our unique, individual gift is an interior one that permeates our whole being and is revealed through the way we live our life.

One way to recognize our gift is through prayer. We need to pray for the gifts of the Spirit and for the ability to discern our particular gift in order to exercise it wisely and fruitfully. In prayer we can reflect on the following:

— In your mind's eye watch yourself doing what you most love to do; pay attention to any images that cross your mind and ponder their meaning. What is the gift you see to be the root of your actions?

— When am I happiest? with whom? doing what? when? where?

— What gives me life? What tires me?

— What do I like? dislike?

— What is my greatest strength? weakness?

— How am I called to exercise my gift in the specific circumstances of my life?

— What are some barriers that keep me from

discovering my gift? from exercising my gift? (Barriers may be internal or external; they may be in the culture, the family, the community or inside a person's feelings or thoughts.)

— What risks will I have to take in order to actualize my gift?

Another way to help discern our gift is to ask others. Often it is others who experience the outpouring of our gift before we are consciously aware of what it is we offer to them. What is it that others seek from us? What do they seem to glean from us and from our presence? Is it peace, love, joy, a renewed spirit, affirmation, a listening heart, consolation, strength in meeting life's challenges? Our gift is something that brings new life to others and to ourselves.

Everyone, including the unlearned, the unskilled, the poor and the handicapped, has a gift to use for the broader community. It has been given, not to be hoarded and guarded, but to be shared with the community for building up the body of Christ and for nourishing and sustaining that body in daily life.

As eucharistic ministers we will find many opportunities for using our gift with those with whom we share the Eucharist. Since it is a gift of the Spirit who is infinite, we will continually discover new ways to exercise it at various times and in various circumstances. Through use our gift will develop and grow. We will be amazed at the ways the Spirit will use us and our gift in leading others to wholeness — and all of us to holiness.

**"Take and Eat"**

# 2
# Prayer

A eucharistic minister went to visit a friend who was dying from a cancerous brain tumor. The two women had frequently prayed the scripture together. The dying woman's love for Jesus was so great that even when she could no longer read because of the tumor's effect on her eyesight, she always had her Bible with her.

"I wonder if Lucy will know me," the minister thought as she approached the hospital. "Her eyesight may be worse, or her faculty for recognition may be impaired."

She entered her friend's room and was stunned when the woman looked at her and joyfully exclaimed, "Jesus!"

Some might think this was definitely a case of mistaken identity. Perhaps. Then, again, it might be that the dying woman was seeing with the eyes of faith, and recognized Christ in her prayerful friend.

Even as the food we eat at a meal becomes part of us physically, we believe that the Eucharist permeates our whole being as well. We are in the process of becoming the spiritual food we eat: Christ himself.

Just as our hunger for food is never satisfied once and for all, neither is our spiritual hunger for God. The members of the body of Christ who are drawn to the eucharistic ministry exhibit a special love and longing for Christ in the Eucharist. Many are able to pray with a community at daily Mass in their parishes or near their place of work. They are also drawn to personal prayer. They hunger for "heavenly bread" and desire to grow in their personal relationship with God. They find that their awareness of God in the events of their daily lives and in the people they meet is increased through the practice of prayer.

## Prayer: Our Relationship With God

In any personal relationship, we continually learn more about each other. Just as we begin to think we know someone well, we discover other aspects we hadn't seen before. If this is true of a relationship with another human being, there is no end to what will be learned in a prayer relationship with an infinite God.

Relationships must change and grow. Parents will relate to their children in different ways as the children grow from infancy into adulthood. Husbands and wives have to go through various stages of growth in their marriage. Friends will experience changes in their relationship.

Our relationship with God will also change and grow as our understanding of God changes. As this happens, we may find that our usual form of prayer doesn't seem to satisfy us. A crisis in our personal lives often precipitates a need to find meanings that only God and faith can provide. We sense that we need to pray differently and desire to do so, yet still may hesitate. Perhaps we don't know any other ways to pray. Or we may experience guilt for what seems to be an abandonment of what has been a familiar and spiritually nourishing form of prayer in the past. Fear, too, can keep us from growth in prayer, for just as we cannot foretell the future of any human relationship, neither can we foretell where our prayer relationship with God will lead. We know what we have, we don't know what may be asked of us if we pray differently. We may wonder if this desire is really a call from God, or merely our own idea.

At a turning point such as this, it is wise to seek out a spiritual director or person of prayer who can be our guide and companion. If this isn't possible, there are many excellent books available that can offer guidance in the search for a meaningful life of prayer.

One way to ascertain whether or not we are being called to deeper prayer is to begin to practice a new form along with the prayer with which we are familiar and then be ready to take a leap of faith when we sense that the time has come to do so.

One minister who was comfortable using words for his prayer began to experience the need for more silent prayer. Not being sure what was happening, but wanting to be open in his response to the Lord, he began to rise 15 minutes earlier in the morning and to spend the time gained sitting silently in the presence of the Eucharistic Christ.

"It was a whole new awareness of God for me. I actually experienced a sense of God's presence in the silence. Sometimes I still use words to pray, but not as many words and not as often as before."

Prayer is first of all an act of praising God and an exercise in self-forgetfulness. It is not a time for self-scrutiny or "navel-gazing," although we may have a lot revealed to us about ourselves during prayer. This doesn't mean we are not aware of our failings and shortcomings, but if we are to become what we pray, we must keep our eyes fixed on God, Jesus, the Holy Spirit.

## Preparation for Prayer

*Time and place*

In making a commitment to prayer, having a set time and a specific place conducive to prayer can help one to enter into prayer more easily. For some, the early morning hours provide the ideal time. The house is still quiet and the routine of the day hasn't begun. For others, the later evening hours are best. For those who find they are frequently awake during the night, using the time for prayer helps to avoid tossing and turning while waiting for sleep to come. The length of time we pray is not as important as our faithfulness to prayer.

An empty room or a quiet corner where one can be undisturbed also facilitates prayer. One eucharistic minister uses her large clothes closet when the family is home and there is little opportunity for privacy anywhere else. Some spiritual guides believe that the place of prayer gradually builds up its own spiritual energy and makes it easier to enter into prayer. They also suggest that places where high energy activity takes place (loud music, a lot of conversation, constant intellectual pursuits) retain the high energy quality and therefore need to be avoided.

Lighting a candle or looking at a favorite picture that draws one to a visual focal point aids in interior focusing and quieting for prayer.

*Fasting*

Another preparation for prayer takes place through various forms of fasting. In a society where the senses are constantly bombarded and stimulated, new forms of fasting can assist us in preparing for and developing our prayer. Some will still feel called to fast from food once a week or once a month in order to facilitate an emptiness and openness to God. Others are becoming more aware of a lack of stillness in their lives and are being more selective about the number of hours and types of TV programs they watch, or radio they listen to, the kind and amount of reading they do, and the number of activities they engage in. In this manner they hope to be more open to the presence and action of God in their lives.

*Beauty*

Taking the time to be immersed in beauty also contributes to one's readiness for prayer. The form beauty takes will vary for each one. For some it may be the enjoyment of an art form: dance, drama, music, painting, sculpture, or literature. For others it may be experienced in nature in a variety of ways: tending a small flower garden, hiking in the woods, climbing a mountain, watching a sunrise or sunset, sitting near a waterfall or running stream, or gazing out over the ocean or a lake.

## Prayer and Personality Types

In recent years research conducted on various personality types (Myers-Briggs Type Indicator) has also shed light on the way individuals prefer to pray. This knowledge has been particularly helpful not only for spiritual guides, but also for those they direct in the life of prayer. In very broad terms, people who are more extroverted usually find themselves drawn to personal prayer that utilizes tangible objects, concrete words and images; in other words, they enter into prayer mostly through their senses. They see God as a person. The more introverted person generally senses God as a presence and prefers silent communication with God, using very little outward stimuli to enter into prayer.

Knowledge of these basic categories can aid in our understanding of why some people are called to one prayer style while others — family members, friends or members of a prayer group — are not comfortable with the same style but prefer a different form of prayer.

The idea of members of the laity being drawn to prayer has seldom been seriously addressed until recent years. The understanding of most people was that only cloistered monks and nuns, removed from everyday life, were called to pray. On the contrary, prayer is not entered into as a way of escaping from reality. Rather it is the means by which we "put on Christ" so that we are permeated with the values of Christ and live these out in daily life. A truly prayerful person, therefore, is very much in tune with the world. He or she challenges others to be aware of God's presence in all of life and "to act justly, to love tenderly, and to walk humbly with your God" (Mi 6:8).

The following pages present a brief explanation of various forms of prayer. It is hoped that those who are interested in one particular form will seek further guidance from a person, a book, or a retreat that is based on that specific type of prayer. The fact that the more familiar forms are not listed is not meant to exclude them as meaningful prayer. The Rosary, litanies and rote prayers are well known to most people and are powerful forms of prayer. They have withstood the test of time. Persons who move into other ways of praying frequently speak of returning to them, especially at times of interior dryness or crisis in their personal lives.

## Personal Prayer

### Scriptural Prayer

Although few of us are called to be scripture

scholars, it can be helpful to our life of prayer if we avail ourselves of opportunities to learn more about the scriptures and the times in which they were written. For that reason, courses in scripture study have become popular in recent years as people begin to experience a hunger for the word of God in the Bible.

Having heard so many homilies and other persons' interpretations of the scriptures in our lifetime, it can be difficult for us to read or hear them read and discover new meanings in them. Yet we can receive fresh insights from praying the scriptures when we bring to them the unique events of our lives. Reading the scriptures with the eyes of faith, we ask, "What is God saying to me in this passage?"

Take time to settle into a comfortable position and relax. Be aware of the presence of a loving God. Begin to slowly read a short scripture passage, either silently or aloud, until a phrase or passage seems to speak to your heart. Then:

— slowly repeat that phrase several times, savoring the living word; or

— talk with God or Jesus about the passage, giving God time to respond in an interior way; or

— enter into the scene and be one of the characters in the particular passage; or

— reflect on the passage in relation to your own life, with its joys and sorrows, peaks and valleys.

Let your response rise up naturally. Be yourself.

The great themes of scripture can also be a source for ongoing prayer, especially at turning points in our lives:

— The call of Abraham (Gn 12), a call to ongoing conversion of heart, can inspire persons of all ages to be open to conversion, to growth in faith in and through their particular life circumstances;

— The exodus journey of Moses (Ex 13,14,15) can sustain us in times of transition in our own lives;

— The desert experience of the Israelites (Ex 16-40) and that of Jesus (Lk 4:1-13; Mt 4:1-11) offers hope at times when we feel cut off from people and things that had previously given meaning to our lives;

— Job (Book of Job), suffering from many losses, including a sense of the presence of God, can sustain us in times of pain, loss and grief;

— Mary's response to God in total faith (Lk

1,2) is a model of faith in our own lives;

— The transfiguration of Christ (Mt 17:1-8) gives us a way to express the joys in our lives as do the many passages on healing (See Appendix I) and the resurrection.

— The eucharistic minister may be led to read and pray scripture passages that specifically refer to the Eucharist (See Appendix I). Some parish communities list in their bulletins the scripture passages for Sunday and each day of the week, or they provide missalettes that give the readings for each day. The *New American Bible* has a list of the Sunday readings for each of the three cycles of the church year listed in the back pages. Praying the scripture reading for the day unites one to the body of Christ in a spiritual way.

## *Keeping a Journal*

For those who like to express themselves through the written word, Journaling is another method of prayer that provides a way to become integrated in one's life — to become whole and holy. Developed by Dr. Ira Progoff, this method teaches how to dialogue with various aspects of one's inner self. The daily spiritual log has proven especially effective as an ongoing framework for prayer. It can be divided into two sections, one for conscious material, the other for unconscious. The individual spends some time each day, or on several days of the week, reflecting on the events of the day. He or she then writes in the section for conscious material how God was experienced in these events, what response was or was not made, what feelings surfaced at the time, and any insights received from the experiences. Eucharistic ministers might look at these events from the perspective of their vocation to be Eucharist for others.

Dreams, fantasies and spontaneous images that come to us at any time are recorded in the section for unconscious material. (Dreams have played a part in Judeao-Christian scriptures from the story of Jacob's dream to the dreams of Joseph in the gospel of Luke.) Resources are also available for those interested in reflecting on their dreams for insights in discerning God's will in their lives.

The effectiveness of the Journaling method is experienced when the individual reads the passages aloud, preferably to an objective listener, a spiritual director, a trusted friend, a prayer partner, a spouse or even to one's self. Only the portions of one's choice from either section need be shared. Somehow the spoken word gives further insight and direction for prayer: for prayer of petition for a needed grace, for praise or thanksgiving to God, for acceptance of God's will in our lives, or for making necessary changes in our lives. Occasionally a day can be set aside for rereading what has been written in the past few days, weeks, or months. The individual then takes time to respond to what has been written during that period of time.

Writing our reflections is a way to search for, and find, the God who dwells within us. We can write freely since no one else will know the contents of our journal unless or until we choose to reveal them.

Two famous "journalists" who have inspired countless people are Pope John XXIII through his *Journal of a Soul* and Dag Hammarskjold, whose journal is entitled *Markings*.

### *Praying With Nature*

Nature offers limitless opportunities for prayer. For some people, just being out in nature is a prayerful experience. Our very being is connected with nature through the food we eat, the water we drink and the air we breathe. A kind of energy is absorbed from nature by those who are attuned to it. They receive a mysterious spiritual renewal and healing from the sights, sounds, smells and touch of God's creation.

Others receive much spiritual benefit from pondering the cycles and processes of nature and their parallels in life: birth, change, death, transformation/resurrection.

In order to experience nature as a form of prayer it isn't imperative that we be in a wilderness setting or even in the country, although these places can heighten our awareness of the presence of God in all of creation. Sitting at a window, watching the birds at a feeder can bring a sense of awe, wonder and praise and can evoke our own response of trust in God. Growing a vegetable or flower garden from seed reminds us that "unless the seed dies, it cannot bear fruit." Seeing the robins return in spring, or hearing the call of migrating geese in the fall keeps one attuned to the cycles of life. We all love spring and summer and the beauty and bounty they bring. Yet fall and winter, times for the earth's resting and renewing, parallel our own need for rest and retreat as well as for productivity.

This may not seem like prayer in comparison to the ways we've prayed in the past. A look at some of the psalms gives evidence that human beings have long been aware of God's presence in nature and have been drawn to praise him therein (Psalms 8,29,67,104,148).

### *Jesus Prayer*

This prayer has a long history, originating in

the scriptural words of the blind man near Jericho: "Jesus, Son of David, have pity on me" (Lk 18:38). The words can be said aloud or even chanted to oneself with as much attention as possible and in coordination with one's breathing: "Jesus, Son of David" while inhaling, "have pity on me" while exhaling. From the beginning of their practice of this prayer, people have become aware of its power. They are led to an awareness of the presence of God within themselves and in the heart of every person. Attitudes are invariably changed as a result of this insight.

*Breathing*

This simple yet powerful form of prayer takes place in the act of becoming aware of one's own breathing. Few of us are ever consciously aware of the vital process of breathing. Over and over again each day we breathe in life and exhale that which is "dead." This is the very life of God in us: "He breathed into his nostrils the breath of life" (Gen 2:7). Being aware of this great gift of the breath of life is prayer. If we choose, we can use a variation of the Jesus Prayer as we breathe: Inhale "Jesus" and exhale "love," "peace," "joy," or any other quality of God we would like to share with the world.

## *Centering Prayer*

This is an ancient contemplative prayer form that has been rediscovered in recent years. It consists of three simple parts:

— Sit relaxed and quiet, aware of God's presence, allowing yourself to be touched by it;

— After a time, a single word may come (or you may choose one): Jesus, God, love, peace, Yahweh. Slowly and effortlessly let yourself repeat this word. Whenever you become aware of any other thought or word, simply replace it by returning to your word;

— When coming out of prayer, move slowly to consciousness of the present; slowly pray the Our Father, savoring each phrase (paraphrased from *Finding Grace at the Center*, edited by Thomas Keating, St. Bede's Publications).

Practice of this prayer two or three times daily for 15 to 20 minutes at a time yields much fruit. Often others are aware of its effect on us before we are ourselves.

In this prayer we can come to experience with God what lovers experience in their relationship with one another. The beloved is always influencing the other's life and is always part of whatever the other is doing. Even when one is not consciously thinking of the beloved, his or her presence is felt.

Distractions will come in any prayer. We're so used to being active that in the beginning it may be hard to be quiet. We may feel the pressure of many duties waiting to be done and a lack of time in which to perform them. Surprisingly enough, we soon find that because we are more centered, composed and at peace, we seem to have more time than before.

### *Art and Creativity as Prayer*

To be in the process of creating a work of art can also be prayer. In the act of painting a picture, dancing, writing a poem, play or book, composing music or playing a musical instrument, sculpting or carving, or producing any other work of art, the artist is a co-creator with God. Similarly, when one is participating in any creative and life-giving outlet and is totally involved in the act, he or she can experience prayer. Homemakers, manual laborers and professionals who enter into their work with enthusiasm and dedicated service are making a prayer of their lives as they too contribute to the building of the kingdom of God.

## Communal Prayer

### *Charismatic Prayer*

As a result of the charismatic renewal, a spiritual movement that began in the '60s and which fosters communal prayer, many prayer groups have sprung up all over the world. Some people, feeling a sense of deprivation in the spiritual dimension of their lives and searching for ways to fill that need, turn to communal prayer. The concern of a caring community touches those individuals who previously have felt isolated in a highly technological world. This care and concern for one another frequently extends beyond the time of prayer, overflowing into many other aspects of daily life. It is not uncommon for members to assist others, in or outside the community, in practical forms of service.

In the setting of a charismatic prayer group, prayers of praise and thanksgiving, scriptural readings, witnessing to God's love and presence in our lives, prayers for healing and of petition, and prayer in the form of singing are all included in the time for prayer.

### *Scriptural Shared Prayer*

In shared prayer those gathered together read the same scripture passage silently. One person then reads it aloud and allows several minutes for silent reflection before inviting the participants to share how they experience the passage in their lives. Each person's response is respected as coming from his or her life of faith and participants refrain from questioning or debating what has been shared. The period of prayer ends with a prayer that is familiar to all.

## *Contemplative Shared Prayer*

In more recent years, individuals as well as members of various prayer groups have found themselves moving toward the prayer of contemplation. Groups are beginning to form to practice this style of silent communing with God.

After a time of physical relaxation done together in silence, the group enters into silent prayer. This may be only 10 minutes to begin with and later may be extended to 20 minutes or longer. When the leader signals the end of silent prayer, the participants slowly come out of prayer, spend a few moments in silent reflection and then either make notes in a journal or rest. The silence is maintained until the leader opens a discussion period of 30 or 40 minutes. The discussion includes the immediate experience of one's day, the practice just experienced and/or the relationship between the two. In closing, intercessory prayer may be offered and a closing prayer or silent gesture (holding hands or the giving of the sign of peace) can be used.

Communal prayer is also practiced in families, in faith-sharing groups that have evolved through the parish-based process of Renew, and by eucharistic ministers who pray with the sick, homebound, hospitalized and residents of nursing homes. "Where two or three are gathered" Jesus is in their midst.

For those who view prayer as a private experience, it may be awkward or embarrassing in the beginning to pray with a group no matter how small in number. Taking the step to overcome one's fears or doubts will be well worth the effort and can lead to a newfound sense of community and church.

## Other Opportunities for Spiritual Growth

Other opportunities for personal and communal spiritual growth that have been available in recent years and are not only enduring the test of time but actually gaining momentum are weekend retreats, Marriage Encounter and the Cursillo movement.

— Weekend retreats provide the time and space for individuals to "come apart and rest awhile." Talks by a retreat leader or team, group sharing, time for solitude and the sacraments of Eucharist and reconciliation usually form the framework for the weekend.

— Marriage Encounter is geared for married couples, but many people who are in relationship in ministry or in friendship have also benefited from the emphasis on, and practice of, honest communication in the context of faith in Jesus Christ. The couples attend a weekend presentation and go through the process that is facilitated by a team made up of married couples and a priest or religious.

— The Cursillo movement, also structured for married couples, will include any other interested party who is sponsored by a previous participant. A husband is asked to participate in the three-day exercise first, while the wife attends the next session for women held a few weeks later. Emphasis is on growth in faith in the Lord and witnessing to the world by one's Christlike life. The leaders are dedicated laity who work with a priest and a religious.

It can be a great help individually and as a community of eucharistic ministers to seek other opportunities to grow in one's love and appreciation for the gift of the Eucharist. These may be initiated on a parish, regional, or diocesan level through means of a Eucharistic Day (a form of what was once known as the Forty Hours Devotion), or a scriptural day of prayer or reflection on the theme of Eucharist. These presentations can be offered in parishes, at retreat houses or spiritual life centers.

## The Fruit of Prayer in Life

Ideally, we eventually come to view all of our life as prayer, for it is in daily life that we continually meet God and give him praise and thanks.

This God who gives himself to us as food, asks us in turn to be food for others in loving service to our brothers and sisters in Christ. We may rejoice or weep and struggle with God, but as we yield our lives in prayer to his all-loving embrace we are being transformed into his image, Jesus Christ. The fruit we manifest as an overflow of our life of prayer — love, joy, peace, patience, kindness, goodness, trustfulness, gentleness and self-control (Gal 5:22-23) — all emerge in our ministry with others. People will recognize them, for "we, with our unveiled faces, reflecting like mirrors the brightness of the Lord, all grow brighter and brighter as we are turned into the image that we reflect; this is the work of the Lord who is Spirit" (2 Cor 3:18).

**"Only Say the Word and I Shall Be Healed"**

# 3
# Pastoral Presence and Skills

In the liturgy just before receiving the body and blood of Christ, the celebrant and community proclaim: "Lord, I am not worthy to receive you, but only say the word and I shall be healed."

By including these words in the liturgy, the church encourages her members to seek healing and new life from the Eucharistic Christ. Paraphrased from the gospel, they are the words of the centurion who asked Jesus to heal his servant while at the same time stating his belief in the power of Jesus to do so (Mt 8:5-13). Jesus was astonished at the faith of someone who was not an Israelite. In other Gospel passages concerning miracles of healing, Jesus also marveled at the faith of the people who came to him.

## Faith of the Minister

It is assumed that the members of the Christian community who have responded to God's call to be eucharistic ministers are also persons of faith who believe in the healing power of the Eucharist. Some participate in daily Mass, finding therein a source of wisdom for the decisions they must make at home or at work. Others receive spiritual strength and support from the whole community gathered for Mass. Those who become ill draw healing comfort and peace from receiving the Eucharist from other ministers.

Early in his public life Jesus went into the synagogue at Nazareth and read from the scroll of Isaiah:

> The Spirit of the Lord has been given to me. . . .
>
> He has sent me to bring the good news to the poor,
>
> to proclaim liberty to captives
>
> and to the blind new sight,
>
> to set the downtrodden free. . . .

Each of these promises can be considered a form of healing and new life. He then proclaimed that the scriptures were being fulfilled now "even as you listen" (Lk 4:18-21). Eucharistic ministers are called to live out this scripture passage today and to be channels of the good news of the healing power of God in the Eucharist and through the witness of their lives.

One minister recognized the healing presence of the Eucharistic Christ during her visits to Mary, an elderly woman in her parish. Mary had left her native Austria as a young woman to act as a governess in the United States. She eventually married and had three children when her husband deserted them. To support herself and the children, Mary worked as a housekeeper and seamstress for many years. Even in her later years she was determined to remain independent and continued to live alone in a tiny apartment in a small village. She took pride in the fact that at the age of 88 she could still go once a week to a nearby nursing home to "help feed the old people." Then she began to experience the mental and physical deterioration that affects some people in their advanced years. Since her parish had recently initiated a eucharistic ministry program, the new minister offered to bring the Eucharist to Mary. She related that several times when she arrived at Mary's apartment, she found her in bed and so weak she could barely speak above a whisper. The minister had given Mary communion and then prepared some soup for her and stayed with her while she ate it. By the time she left a short while later, Mary was much stronger and able to function again. Reflecting on the experience, the minister said, somewhat in awe, "I think that the spiritual and physical nourishment, together with the stimulation of another person's presence, probably all played a part in the change I saw take place in that short time."

## Hope of the Minister

At the beginning of Jesus' public ministry, John the Baptist called him the "Lamb of God, who takes away the sins of the world."

The effect of sin is only too evident in the sufferings of daily life. Jesus as the innocent and trusting Lamb of God confronted sin, yet willingly accepted the painful aspects of life. He did this not masochistically or stoically, but simply because he knew they were part of life. He accepted suffering and death, and transformed them through his own transforming resurrection. He diffused their power to enslave and infused them with his power for new life. Because of our hope in Christ and this power for new life, we as Christians are challenged to look at suffering in a different light and find in it a mysterious means of transformation in our own lives. When suffering takes on this different meaning, one that cannot be destroyed by outward appearances, we are able to continue to hope in the promises of the risen Christ.

The eucharistic minister who views life from a Christian perspective seems to have a more positive attitude and lives out of a framework of hope. To become aware of your own attitude, look at the way you interact with others.

— What is it you talk about: persons? places? events? ideas?

— How do you perceive what is happening in your life and in the lives of those around you? Do you label them as "good" or "bad" according to the way you feel about them? How do you communicate these perceptions to others?

— What is your basic attitude as you talk: a constructive one of "building up" or a destructive one of "tearing down"?

— Do you find yourself uplifted or depressed, peaceful or disturbed after your conversations?

If you find that you frequently communicate negative thoughts, ideas and fears, realize that this is a reaction to the outer circumstances of the moment. If in faith you are able to look beyond appearances, to see them from a spiritual viewpoint and to concentrate on positive expressions or interpretations—as good news—you are developing an attitude of hope.

For the minister who professes to believe in the good news of the gospel, it is important to maintain this hopeful attitude and to recognize when you are being drawn into cynicism or yielding to negative reactions or attitudes. This does not mean that you deny, ignore, or minimize the sufferings of life in a Pollyanna fashion, but that you refuse to give them power over your life. Many of the situations we've learned to label as "bad" or "terrible" at the time we experience them eventually are found to contain a hidden blessing as well.

A personal prayer life can be a powerful asset here. Those who spend time in prayer often come to the realization that these painful events can provide the opportunity for spiritual, psychological, or emotional healing and growth to take place in unexpected ways.

To sustain this hopeful attitude, eucharistic ministers might consider doing one or more of the following:

— joining with others to form a faith-sharing community that will offer prayer support;
— cultivating friends who reinforce this virtue;

— offering prayers of thanksgiving for blessings received as well as praying for needs.

Christ is our model for hope. We see this hope expressed in the liturgy in the words of the acclamation after the consecration: "Christ has died, Christ is risen, Christ will come again." While the words "Christ will come again" certainly refer to the final coming of Christ, they can also be interpreted to mean that, since Christ lives on, he comes again in our lives today. The hopeful eucharistic minister is a sign of this coming. Meeting a person of hope, one who projects a positive attitude toward life and who seems not only to believe in but also to live out the good news, conveys hopefulness to other people as well. This hopefulness is yet another aspect of the healing ministry of Christ.

## Love of the Minister

In John's gospel Christ refers to himself as the good shepherd who is willing to lay down his life for his sheep. The pastoral scene he describes (Jn 10) conveys the love and compassion of the shepherd for the sheep who depend on him for their well-being and safety. Throughout his life, Jesus gave of himself to those who needed him, especially the sick, the weak, the outcast, the poor. He shared their lives, rejoiced with them and wept with them. Eventually he gave his life for all.

Since Vatican Council II there has been a renewal of this pastoral mission of Christ in his church. Those called to be ministers of the Eucharist participate in this healing mission of love, compassion and care for others by being willing to reach out to the suffering body of Christ and to help its members bear their burdens. The ministers have various and sometimes unsuspected powers for healing through their unique personalities and spiritual gifts. Most think of themselves as very ordinary people and seldom realize that their very presence can be a source of healing. While we've been accustomed to think of healing only in physical terms, Christ offers many forms of healing through his ministers.

— Some relate to the sick and homebound in a way that consoles and comforts them. When an individual says, "I feel better since you've come," they are actually saying that a form of healing has occurred.

— Others are good at listening and frequently hear, "Just being able to talk with you has been a help to me."

— Some eucharistic ministers share a common ethnic heritage and understand the sick or homebound individual in a way no one else can. In the case of a few of the elderly who only speak their native language, the ministers can meet a great need especially in hospitals or nursing homes. When a eucharistic minister of Italian descent arrived in the hospital room of an elderly patient, he found that the woman had just fallen. As the orderlies prepared to take her for X-rays, the patient was speaking in Italian. The minister realized that she was asking God to help her. He spoke to the woman in Italian, asking if she'd like to receive the Eucharist before going for X-rays. The woman's face lit up and she responded by saying this was an answer to her prayer. While seemingly a small incident, it was obvious to the minister that it provided consolation for the woman.

— Eucharistic ministers who are parents and whose children accompany them when they bring communion to the homebound offer a unique gift to those who have little opportunity to see children. Parents often hear, "We do so enjoy having the children come. Please bring them again." They are frequently amazed at the close bond that develops between the older and younger generations.

— The warm and welcoming smile of the eucharistic minister who serves communion in church may be just the healing gift needed by one who lives alone, or by another who may be feeling a bit lonely that day.

— Some eucharistic ministers have the gift of healing touch, develop it through prayer and meditation and quietly use it in their visits to the sick and homebound. Laying their hands on the head of the one who is in pain or experiencing anxiety transmits a warmth that is sometimes felt physically and often relieves the pain or anxiety. Then, too, a handclasp, an arm around someone's shoulders, or even a hug of greeting or farewell is often more needed and welcomed than one realizes. Persons who live alone and who have no close relatives seldom experience this gift of a physical touch. I recall visiting a nursing home a few years ago and putting my arm around the shoulders of a woman who was seated near me. She responded immediately, drawing me close to her and placing her head against mine. I realized for the first time the need the elderly have for a caring human touch.

The sick and homebound recognize the selflessness of those who bring the Eucharist. They are deeply touched and grateful for the fact that people whom they do not know personally, but who share a common faith, are willing and eager to reach out to them. Knowing that others care enough about them to bring them the Eucharist and to spend time with them, greatly enhances their self-esteem. This in itself is a means of healing, especially at a time when much of society seems to consider them useless because they are no longer "productive" members.

## Developing Pastoral Skills for Healing

As they grow in their love for the Eucharist and continue in their ministry to others, eucharistic ministers will begin to realize the way Christ touches others in a healing way through them. Their ministry can become more effective as they learn and develop some pastoral skills for facilitating healing. These skills will be rooted in prayer and based on self-knowledge, knowledge of techniques for listening and relating to others, and trust in the Holy Spirit for wisdom and guidance.

### *Empathy, Not Sympathy*

How often we hear the words, "Oh I feel so sorry for her." We may even spontaneously express them ourselves as we see or hear of someone experiencing one of life's difficult or painful situations: a long term illness, a sudden death, a separation or divorce, the loss of employment, and so on. The reaction is an honest one and the fact that we are moved by another's pain shows that the seeds of compassion and caring are within us. In reflecting on the effect another's pain has on us, we realize that it forces us to look at how vulnerable each one of us can be in similar circumstances. When these times come, the compassionate and caring person can be a lifeline in dealing with them and in moving beyond them to healing and new life.

Webster defines sympathy as "sameness of feeling; affinity between persons or of one person for another." When both parties remain on the feeling level, however, there is little or no opportunity for one to offer the kind of assistance that has long-term results. The message that is sometimes conveyed from a feeling of sympathy is that of pity, a pity that may regard the other as too weak or lacking the necessary inner resources to handle the present situation. At such times, the sympathetic person may rush to the rescue, either verbally with a lot of well-intentioned, but often useless advice, or by performing services that can unconsciously convey the message: "You're not able to take care of this now, so I'll have to do it for you." (In some situations the latter may be true, but except for rare instances, for example, a person in extreme depression or those who are severely handicapped, this is usually only temporary.)

Empathy, on the other hand and again according to Webster, is "the projection of one's own personality into the personality of another in order to understand him/her better; intellectual identification of one's self with another."

The difference lies between the emotional and intellectual dimensions of the two personalities and the ways they are expressed. The empathic person may deeply feel another's pain, but is able to move out of the feeling level and maintain an intellectual objectivity both in perspective and involvement. Recognizing that everyone goes through painful experiences in life and that these can be a means of growth, the empathic eucharistic minister supports the person who is suffering with prayer for him or her, and by listening with an objectivity that points out alternate ways of seeing or doing. This allows others to draw on latent strengths and capabilities for solving their own problems, thereby enabling them to maintain a sense of autonomy and self-esteem.

This empathic approach is more in keeping

with the attitude of Christ who gave others the freedom to be themselves and to make their own choices even when these didn't always seem to be in their best interests — the rich young man, for example. At the same time he challenged others to do something about changing their situation: Zacchaeus, the man at the Pool of Bethesda. In empathy, eucharistic ministers help others to carry the cross of Christ; they don't attempt to carry it for them.

## Silent Presence

There are times when words are either inappropriate or unnecessary. Someone who is seriously ill or dying seldom has either the energy or the desire for conversation. If after giving them the Eucharist the minister can sit with them in silence for a few minutes, perhaps holding their hand and praying silently, the healing of the Eucharistic Christ can be communicated through caring presence.

Anyone who is going through a traumatic experience also needs the silent support of an understanding heart and a listening ear, rather than pious referrals to "God's will" or the "merit of suffering." An understanding of the meaning of suffering for the one undergoing it must ultimately come from within.

One eucharistic minister related her experience in the following words: "I think of a lady who is the victim of a stroke. She recently lost a small grandchild, a son and her husband of more than 50 years. She has a need to talk about them and times gone by. To listen is all one can do, and it is enough. It relieves her loneliness. I see her smiling face still at the door as I drive away, and know her day is complete. Somehow, so is mine."

By sharing the Eucharist and listening in silence, ministers can communicate their care and facilitate the healing process. In listening to feelings of sorrow or guilt, or by hearing about memories from the past, they enable the person who is suffering to experience a healing catharsis.

## *Listening*

One of the most effective gifts for healing is listening. To be a pastoral listener involves more than just not speaking; there is an active participation that is needed as well. Allowing another to express painful feelings or ugly moods makes room for the Spirit of God to enter in and transform the ugliness to beauty, the darkness to light. While not being expected to take on the role of professional counselor, having a basic knowledge of pastoral listening skills can enable eucharistic ministers to offer this gift to others if they desire to do so.

*Remote Preparation*

Before visiting the homebound or hospitalized, pray that you will be able to hear more than just the words that are spoken aloud; pray you will recognize Christ in the other person and be inspired as to what to do or say as you listen.

Realize that eucharistic communion opens the way for another kind of communion, when a heart that is hurting can entrust you with confidence and find healing in your ability to listen.

Ask yourself what your expectations are when you listen to others. Do you feel you must solve their problems, take away their pain, or help them feel better? Any one of these may happen, but this is not your responsibility as a listener.

*Active Listening*

1. On entering the hospital room or the home of the person with whom we are to share the Eucharist, the question "How are things going today?" rather than the conventional "How are you?" gives the person an opening to share concerns and feelings. People have few chances to share their feelings with others who show they care and who will not judge them for the way they feel or think. Even when you may not agree with the values or approach to life of the other person, you can still show that you accept

and value him or her as a son or daughter of God.

One eucharistic minister had made several visits to a hospitalized man. Each time the man refused communion. On the sixth visit, the patient looked at the minister and said, "I think you really do care about me. Come in." He received communion and spent some time sharing his concerns with the minister.

2. To show that you are willing to be actively involved in the listening process, be seated if possible while the other is speaking. Standing over a person conveys the sense that you are in a hurry. Face others and look at them as they speak, giving them your undivided attention.

3. Occasionally reflect back what you've heard them say. If you haven't heard them correctly, they will usually tell you. Many times people will suddenly "see" what they're saying and realize what they need to do next or how to accept what lies ahead for them. An occasional nod, an appropriate comment or an understanding look lets them know you hear more than just the words they are speaking — you hear their pain or concern as well.

4. Ask questions that help them express their feelings:

"How did you feel about that?"

"It sounds to me as though you felt (angry, sad, upset . . . ) when that happened, is that right?"

"Can you say more about that?"

"Oh?" (This simple word, expressed as a question, is very effective in inviting people to say more about whatever is on their minds.)

If you don't understand what they are saying, ask them to try to tell you in different words, or ask them for an example of what they mean.

Refrain from asking questions merely out of curiosity.

5. Never tell a person, "Don't feel that way." We are all powerless to change the way we feel. Recall how you've felt if or when someone has said the same thing to you.

6. If you are asked your opinion, by all means express it, but only as an opinion, not as the only or best way to deal with whatever situation has been revealed to you. Ask the other person what options he or she sees. Asking questions rather than making statements helps people ponder alternate ways of looking at and solving their difficulties. ("Have you thought of . . . ? Have you tried . . . ?")

*Supportive Listening*

In supportive listening, the listener shows by a nod, an understanding look or a brief comment or response that he or she is hearing what the other person is saying. One way to do this is to simply comment, "It's kind of hard to talk about that, isn't it?" when it appears obvious that this is so. The other knows that you realize the pain or embarrassment he or she is experiencing.

People are often unaware that agencies exist to help meet a variety of needs. In situations where there is a need for professional counseling or practical assistance, you can help by knowing what agencies provide the necessary services. If you are unfamiliar with such agencies, ask someone on the church staff for information or call the social services department in your area to find out what is available. Have the person in need make the request unless it is absolutely impossible for him or her to do so. Sometimes we may see what we believe to be a need, while the person either does not want help, is unable to recognize a need for assistance, may feel unable to afford it, or may even be resistant to it since it may necessitate life changes.

If someone feels free to cry in your presence, consider yourself privileged to be allowed to witness and share in the person's pain. To quickly console someone who cries or insist he or she not cry because we're uncomfortable with tears is to deny an opportunity for healing.

*Listening to the Depressed Person*

When ministering to depressed persons, however, it's better not to let them dwell on their problems, since doing so tends to lead them further into depression. Try instead to help them identify the resources and personal strengths they do have and ways they can use them to find possible solutions for their perceived problems. This is more constructive and active than focusing on feelings which only become overwhelming in this instance. Suggest that they consult their doctor if they haven't already done so. In some persons, depression has been known to be caused by a physical condition.

*Listening to the Chronic Complainer*

In the course of your ministry, you may occasionally be asked to bring the Eucharist to individuals who are chronic complainers. They either have no intention of taking any steps to resolve their problems, or may simply lack the inner resources or motivation to do so. Eucharistic ministers will need to protect themselves from the emotional overload directed at them and to help in a concrete way if possible. A few practical suggestions may be of some help:

1. Pray for them. It may or may not change them, but we may find our own attitude toward them changing and we'll be better able to minister with compassion and empathy.

2. Help the complainers to identify their strengths, and ask leading questions so they can find answers for themselves:

"I see you have a new (walker, cane, wheelchair, etc.). What things can you do now that you couldn't do before?"

"Did you say (name of individual) helps you by (bringing your groceries, mowing your lawn, raking the leaves, doing your banking, etc.)?"

"I understand new benefits are available for people in situations similar to yours. How will this help you?"

It may take a lot of ingenuity to think of something, but it will help the other to realize that you are not going to give misplaced sympathy. It will also help you maintain a healthy psychological distance and not allow the other to take control in a way that is not helpful for either of you.

3. Limit your time with complainers. It may be difficult to leave when the other person never seems to have finished a list of complaints or tale

of woe. For those who have been taught to "be polite," to "respect your elders," or who get caught in sympathizing with the other, it may be extremely difficult to kindly but firmly take control of the situation. Conduct the service and leave as soon after as possible.

*Obstacles to Listening*

There are times and circumstances that may make listening difficult or next to impossible.

**Lack of time.** You may simply not have the time to listen to someone on a given day. If you can and want to do so, present the person with an alternative. A simple statement, "I have another commitment right now, but I can come back later/tomorrow/before the week is over . . . if you like." Even an offer of a phone conversation is better than no opportunity for follow up. If the situation occurs in the course of your ministry in the hospital, you might offer to inform the chaplain and ask him or her to stop by later. If the person agrees to your suggestion, be sure you give the message to the chaplain.

**Unmet personal needs.** Preoccupation with an urgent need of your own or of a family member may make it difficult to listen to the needs of another. At such times, it is better not to provide the opening for another to talk with you about a serious matter.

***Painful topic.*** The subject the other needs to talk about may be a difficult one for you to listen to: widowhood, bereavement, terminal illness. If you haven't faced some of these issues yourself, you may experience feelings of fear or anxiety and be unable to listen effectively. If you have just gone through a similar experience or are facing it in the near future, it may be too painful to listen well. Respect your own needs and realize this is not a failure on your part.

***Distractions.*** Many things may happen that make it difficult to listen: the loud TV of a nearly deaf roommate in a hospital or nursing home; the confusion of a busy household where a homebound person resides; frequent interruptions on the part of attendants in a hospital. If the person is ambulatory, you might try to find another place to talk.

***A need to rescue the other.*** If a sense of our own worth hinges on our being able to change others or "save" them from a painful situation, we will be unable to listen effectively. Our mind will be too busy trying to find solutions for them.

The most difficult obstacles to overcome are those that may reside in ourselves: impatience with the sick or elderly, a judgmental attitude, an argumentative nature. If these are part of us, we may need to acknowledge the fact and not try to do what we are unable to do until, or unless, there is a change in us. There are other gifts we do have and can give to those we visit with the Eucharist.

## *Healing for Those Who Grieve*

While grief is a common experience for all people, it is also unique for each one. Ever since Elisabeth Kubler-Ross researched and wrote *On Death and Dying*, much has been learned about the stages of grieving undergone by the person facing imminent death. In recent years, it has been noted that not only the dying go through these stages. Anyone who suffers a loss of any kind may also undergo a similar grieving process.

Those who are ill have lost their health. Some may have lost a limb, an organ of the body or some bodily function through surgery. Sickness and aging may change the usual relationship between spouses. One 90-year-old woman whose husband had become mentally confused sadly told the minister who brought communion, "He never calls me by my name anymore."

Homebound persons may have lost their health. Those who are older may be widowed as well. Both the sick and homebound have lost mobility and control over their own lives to a greater or lesser degree.

Persons in any of these situations need time and support to work through denial, anger, bargaining, depression and acceptance. The eucharistic minister who can spend time with the grieving person after the eucharistic service can draw on and continue the healing power of the Eucharist through pastoral concern and skills. Having some knowledge of the process of grieving as well as specific ways to offer help at this time will help minimize the minister's own feelings of helplessness or apprehension.

The following are ways the grieving process manifests itself and some specific suggestions for the minister who wishes to help the grieving person.

*Denial* is an intellectual barrier set up to ward off the pain that accompanies any loss. Persons in this phase need to build up inner resources before facing and acknowledging the loss. They may be in shock and exhibit what seems to be inappropriate behavior: loud laughter, overactivity, crying jags, possessiveness of personal property, talking about a deceased person or a former situation as though the loss had never occurred. The eucharistic minister who realizes what is happening will not try to force the other to face reality. On an intellectual level grieving persons know the facts, but on the feeling level they are not ready to accept them. Your visits and ability to listen will show that you care and won't judge or avoid them. Let them talk about their loss. Even though they say the same thing over and over again, know that doing so gradually relieves the pain for them. Give practical support whenever possible: a helpful book, a shared task or errand performed, a meal prepared and shared. Avoid pity and treat the person as normally as possible. If a spouse or other relative or friend has died and you knew him or her, share the good things you remember.

*Anger* may erupt at the most unexpected times and seemingly for the most insignificant reason or for no apparent reason at all. People's anger may be directed at doctors or at themselves for a supposed failure to prevent the loss, at another whom they perceive to have been responsible in some way for their present situation, or at God who let it happen. The eucharistic minister helps the individual through this phase by letting the anger be verbalized and preventing it from being turned inward where ultimately it does more harm. Remember that anger is a feeling and not a rational reaction to the loss. Tears are sometimes a release of anger; allowing the person to cry aids in dissipating anger.

*Bargaining* consists of a promise (usually made to God) to do or accept something in exchange for more time before the loss becomes permanent. "If I can just see my granddaughter married before . . . " or "I only want to get to my son's graduation before (such and such happens) then I'll be ready to. . . . " Often if the desired event does take place, another one is held up for bargaining. The eucharistic minister who can listen and refrain from forcing realistic views on the grieving, or from depriving them of hope, gives them a chance to talk about their hopes and pain and ultimately to accept reality.

*Depression* is probably the hardest phase to deal with both on the part of depressed people and the ministers who bring the Eucharist. The grieving understand now that they cannot change the course of events. They feel overwhelmed with grief; their outlook often becomes pessimistic, their mannerisms change, as does their normal routine. Many depressed persons sleep a lot, thereby avoiding the pain they feel when awake. At this stage, eucharistic ministers must avoid trying to "jolly" depressed people out of their depression and show their affection and concern in little ways: a phone call, a note or card between visits, a simple squeeze of the hand, or a hug with no words spoken at all may suffice and assure depressed individuals that they are not alone. All of these say, "I care," or "I'm sorry."

At the same time eucharistic ministers

need to be aware of the way depression can be transmitted to them. This is the time to develop one's ability for empathy and to avoid being caught up in sympathy. Brief visits or contacts are more apt to contribute toward healing and at the same time prevent the depression from being transferred to the minister.

*Acceptance* comes when one has been allowed to go through the other stages. It brings some semblance of peace to those who are grieving. Gradually they feel able to be more involved in their own life and in the lives of others again. They begin once more to make small decisions and choices for themselves and become better adjusted to new routines, changed circumstances and lifestyle. They may still experience one or more of the other aspects of grief on occasion, but on the whole they've worked through the worst part.

As in all movements of the Spirit, there is no set time for all of this to be accomplished, nor is there any one way that it happens. It will be different for each person. For the eucharistic minister who has been willing to help others through this painful time in their lives, there will be rejoicing and gratitude that they have been chosen to assist their suffering brothers and sisters and have played a part in their healing.

## Needs of the Minister

### Need to Grieve

In the desire and willingness to meet the needs of others, it is important that we recognize our own needs as well. We, too, experience loss and are affected when those with whom we have shared the Eucharist move away, become more feeble or die. We needn't be ashamed to let our own emotions surface and to express the pain we feel in order to experience healing ourselves. In a society that tends to suppress pain and to deny the reality of death, it is important that we as Christians acknowledge and accept them as part of life and faith.

Eucharistic ministers who visit the sick and homebound will have more experiences of loss and grieving than other members of the Christian community. One minister had been bringing communion to the homebound members of her parish for several years and had kept a list of all those she had visited during that time.

"The other day, I was going over my list," she remarked, "and I realized that almost all of the people had either died or gone into a nursing home. Only one had moved away. It's painful to have people come into your life and then, when you've come to know and love them, go out of it again."

*Need to Process Experience*

Eucharistic ministers who experience significant losses in their ministry as they try to provide a pastoral healing presence for others need to take time to process their experiences.

- Someone on the parish staff might be available to facilitate a group dealing specifically with loss and grief, or be available to individual eucharistic ministers when they need to discuss the impact their ministry has on them.
- A parishioner who is a trained counselor may be willing to give some time on a monthly or bimonthly basis to facilitate such a group for eucharistic ministers.
- The diocese can be asked to identify speakers, programs, or resources that are available for ongoing education.
- A counseling center can provide guidelines for group interaction and support or can train someone to facilitate a group.
- The pastoral care departments in most hospitals have chaplains available to offer support to the ministers as well as to patients. Those that have training programs for ministers usually include suggestions for ways that ministers can recognize and meet some of their own needs.

Besides being familiar with social service agencies, it is helpful if eucharistic ministers know what services their own parishes offer for their sick and homebound members, especially those who have no family nearby. Knowing that others can supplement their spiritual service with practical assistance as well relieves ministers of taking on responsibilities they may be unable to meet. Other members of the faith community are often willing to help if they are made aware of specific needs. Some parishioners may offer transportation for appointments or errands; others work to provide emergency food or clothing for those on a limited income. Others visit the homebound and read to parishioners who can no longer see, or write letters for those unable to do so. Confirmation candidates who are involved in service programs can offer to do yard work or light housekeeping, run errands or visit elderly parishioners. The eucharistic community that combines faith with good works is one that thereby provides mutual support for all its members.

### *Need to Receive Gift of Others*

As eucharistic ministers, we need to resist the temptation to be always the ones who give. The person with whom we share the Eucharist also needs to give to us in some way.

The sick and homebound give of their hospitality in welcoming us into their home or hospital or nursing home room. They give their appreciation for being able to receive their Eucharistic Lord. They give the witness of their faith, fortitude, patience and courage in the face of suffering. Those who have aged gracefully offer the wisdom of their experience of life. Some appreciate being able to give a small homemade gift in gratitude for your ministry and friendship. It could be hurtful and insulting to them not to accept and exchange a small gift at Christmastime or when either party is celebrating a birthday or anniversary.

Sometimes the gift that is given meets a personal spiritual need. One minister whose husband had just been diagnosed with a terminal illness was assigned to bring the Eucharist to an older woman who was also terminally ill. The sick woman spoke openly of her illness and the way she was preparing to die. The peace she obviously possessed impressed the eucharistic minister and she in turn was able to talk about her husband's illness. Later the minister spoke of this as being a great help to her as she and her husband went through their own grieving process.

## *Need to Recognize and Accept Limitations*

At different times in life, we all experience a sense of our limitations or weaknesses, whether they be of time, energy, knowledge, skills, or the wisdom needed to help someone else. Eucharistic ministers may experience one or more of these limitations and weaknesses in visiting the sick and homebound with the Eucharist. While we may have the mobility and health they do not have, we nevertheless are often powerless to help sick or homebound persons either to change the situation they are in or to adjust to it. At such times we may feel we are doing little or nothing for them. While this can be a source of pain for the caring person, it is also an opportunity to reflect on the words of scripture, "My grace is enough for you: my power is at its best in weakness" (2 Cor 12:9). This paradox can never be totally understood, but we can catch glimpses of its meaning through prayerful reflection on our own lives and the lives of those around us:

— Eucharistic ministers who have known the pain of loss of a loved one are often the best source of comfort for those experiencing a similar loss.

— Those who have undergone rehabilitation for addictions and are recovering have the most credibility in their outreach to others who are just beginning their journey back to wholeness.

— The physically handicapped live with their limitations each day, and yet are frequently a source of inspiration and encouragement to all with whom they minister.

— Many older people experience the limitations of aging. Those who are eucharistic ministers need to realize that their very willingness to serve as ministers is a tremendous witness of love and selflessness to the rest of the parish community.

Somehow our very weaknesses are the channel through which the power of God can flow! Therefore, everyone can find hope in the words of Paul: "So I shall be very happy to make my weaknesses my special boast so that the power of Christ may stay over me. . . . For it is when I am weak that I am strong" (2 Cor 12:9-10). It is the power of the Eucharistic Christ who brings healing through the sacrament and the very weaknesses of the ministers.

## "Do This in Memory of Me"

# 4
# Practical Guidelines

The eucharistic minister, as a disciple of Christ today, is called to represent Christ to others and to serve him at the liturgy, in homes, hospitals and nursing homes. As disciples, eucharistic ministers are the word, the Eucharist, the love of God for others given in a practical as well as spiritual way. Through them the church reaches out to include all her people: those who are present at the liturgy and those who are unable to be physically present with the rest of the community.

## Preparation for Service

There are several ways to facilitate ongoing formation and immediate preparation for ministry. Some have already been mentioned: the desire and love for the Eucharist, the desire to share this love with others, perseverance in personal prayer, a sensitivity to the needs of others and an effort to exhibit a hopeful attitude and a caring manner. In addition, many eucharistic ministers find it enriching to read the scriptures chosen by the church for each day of the year. Others read the scriptures for the forthcoming Sunday early in the week. As the week progresses, they are aware of the ways the word of God is present in their daily lives. As they participate in the liturgy on Sunday and hear the scriptures read, the words take on new meaning for them. Still others take extra time for prayer on the day they are to engage in their ministry, praying especially for the needs of the people they will visit that day. They are aware of their role as Christ's disciples and prepare accordingly.

Ordinarily before anyone takes on a new endeavor in life, he or she first finds out as much as possible about the requirements involved in terms of personal qualities and/or talents needed, what is entailed in carrying out the responsibilities, how much time is involved and what some of the personal rewards might be. This is no less true for the Christian who is called to be a eucharistic minister.

Usually there are four areas of eucharistic

sharing on the parish level. Each one requires general as well as specific guidelines for facilitating ministry. Having some knowledge of these can be a helpful beginning in choosing one's area of service.

## Service at Liturgy

### Knowing the Procedures

Eucharistic ministers will find that knowing the specific procedures the parish has adopted for distributing communion during the liturgy will help them to feel at ease as well as contribute to the smooth progression of the liturgy. These may be spelled out at an educational session prior to the minister being commissioned, or written out and distributed to each one, or posted in the church sacristy.

In most places of worship, the ministers are encouraged to sit near the front of the church. This enables them to come from the community and to move easily into the sanctuary.

Usually the ministers go to the altar at the words: "Lamb of God. . . ." They may receive the host from the celebrant and then communicate all together when he does, or receive from him after he has communicated. Those serving the body of Christ receive from the cup next, then take their dish (or ciborium) and go to their assigned places. Those serving the precious blood drink from the cup and then take it to their assigned places.

### *Conveying a Hospitable Manner*

In sharing the body and blood of Christ an attitude of hospitality such as one would exhibit in welcoming guests into your home is of the utmost importance. Ask yourself: What would I wear if Christ were coming to my home? How would Christ speak the words, and how would he greet and relate to his people? As each person comes to you, hold the host or cup at or near your eye level while saying, "The Body (or Blood) of Christ." In this way you can look the person in the eye and smile in welcome. Saying the person's name if you know it is another way of personalizing the action. In the beginning nervousness may cause a tendency to hurry the process. By taking your time with each one, you can overcome some of the anxiety that is normally experienced when anyone begins something new.

### *What to Do . . .*

If you need more hosts or wine:

If you find that you won't have enough hosts or wine for all the communicants, you can either go to another minister (or to the tabernacle) for more hosts, or to the altar for more wine. If the communicant receives only the body or blood of Christ, our faith tells us that they have still received the fullness of the sacrament.

If the Eucharist is dropped or spilled:

Sometimes at a meal, food is dropped or a beverage is spilled. So, too, at the eucharistic meal. If this happens, there is no need to panic. Reverence for the Eucharist is to be desired, but not exaggerated. If a host is dropped, pick it up and put it aside on the plate you are using (or hold it in the hand that is holding the ciborium containing the other hosts). After you finish distributing communion, you can break it up and put it in the sacrarium, a special sink usually located in the sacristy that empties directly into the ground instead of into the sewage system. If the precious blood is spilled, position yourself so that no one will step in it during the rest of the time of communion. Then, as soon as possible, wipe it up with the cloth purificator you've been using for the cup. If the purificator is saturated, rinse it out and drain the water in the sacrarium. Otherwise it can be put in the specified place.

If you have doubts about the person receiving:

On rare occasions you may find yourself in the position of offering the Eucharist to someone whom you have reason to believe is not in good standing with the church. What course of action is to be taken in such a situation? Since no one can know the state of another person's conscience and relationship with God, it isn't your role to act as judge. You can give such people the Eucharist in good faith, since the responsibility is theirs not yours. If you find this difficult, you may need to discuss your dilemma with a priest.

When all communicants have received, the ministers take any remaining hosts or wine to the tabernacle. Usually if any of the precious blood is still left, it is consumed by the ministers at the tabernacle or in the sacristy. The remaining hosts are placed in one (or more if needed) ciborium in the tabernacle and the empty dishes are then put in the designated place in the sacristy. The cups are rinsed and dried before being put away. Normally the water from this washing is poured into the sacrarium.

If for any reason you are not going to be able to be present at the liturgy for which you are assigned to serve communion, be sure you either get a substitute or notify the person in charge of the ministry. The exception would be a last-minute emergency over which you have no control.

## Conducting Paraliturgical Services

As the number of ordained clergy declines, we are beginning to witness more eucharistic ministers involved as leaders of paraliturgical communion services. This has been viewed with regret and dismay by some, with hope and expectation by others. Believing this to be a new movement of the Spirit in the church, calling forth the gifts of those baptized into Christ the Eucharistic Lord, has enabled many to accept and welcome the change.

The paraliturgical rite of distributing communion outside of Mass follows the same basic format that is used in bringing communion to the homebound: a greeting, penitential rite, scripture readings of the day, prayer of the faithful, the reception of Holy Communion and a concluding rite. Hymns may be sung before and after the service as well as during communion, especially if the number to receive is fairly large.

## Ministry of the Handicapped

In some parishes, the physically handicapped are welcomed and encouraged to become ministers of the Eucharist. Someone in a wheelchair who has the use of arms and hands can distribute the body or blood of Christ in church, although they may require some assistance in obtaining the dish or cup. Others who may not feel comfortable serving the Eucharist in church are able to go to hospitals or nursing homes that are accessible to the handicapped. One young woman in her 20s who is paralyzed from the waist down as the result of an accident not only serves the Eucharist in her parish church but for several years went once every three weeks to a local rehabilitation hospital where she herself had been hospitalized. The patients there were both inspired and encouraged by her cheerfulness, sense of humor and deep faith.

## Service to the Homebound

### *Re-membering Those Not Present*

A special ministry of the eucharistic community is the ministry to the homebound. Sunday after Sunday in many parishes eucharistic ministers leave the church after Mass to bring communion to the members of their parish who are homebound and who have expressed a desire to receive their Eucharistic Lord. As a representative of the local church, the eucharistic minister is helping to "re-member" the homebound person as part of the worshiping community, that is, to call to mind their presence in such a way that even though they are not actually present with the community, they are present in a spiritual way. They are thereby included in the community even when circumstances prohibit their physical presence. Some celebrants offer a commissioning prayer at the end of Mass for ministers who are going to the homebound, thus reminding the gathered community of the homebound members who are not able to be present.

In some parishes, retired and/or widowed persons who are eucharistic ministers bring communion during the week to members of the parish who are temporarily homebound because of surgery, an accident or, in the case of the elderly, inclement weather. One person can coordinate this ministry for those who request it.

### *The Homebound Person*

The homebound are not necessarily only the older members of a parish who are ill or too feeble to leave their homes. They might also include a young person suffering from a crippling or terminal disease, someone with a serious heart condition, or an individual suffering from multiple sclerosis, muscular dystrophy, rheumatoid arthritis, or cancer. All have one thing in common: their love and appreciation for their Eucharistic Lord. Most of them exhibit tremendous faith and courage as they live their lives isolated from the community and/or in physical pain a great deal of the time.

Almost without exception, the ministers relate the experience of receiving much more than they give. One young couple with two small daughters, ages four and seven, experienced being ministered to on their first visit to an elderly, severely handicapped woman. Their older daughter had recently begun to use the phrase "I can't" when asked to try something new. The parents had tried unsuccessfully to curb the habit before it became too ingrained. During the communion call with the whole family present the woman, who lived alone and obviously had great difficulty getting about, shared a bit of her story. She ended by saying, "And I have never let the words 'I can't' become part of my vocabulary." The parents in total amazement glanced at their daughter who, even at her young age, could comprehend what that must mean.

"From that day on," the parents reported, "we've seldom heard the words, 'I can't,' and if any one of us uses them, the others are quick to remind him or her of our valiant friend."

The appreciation extended by the homebound, as well as their prayer and love, far exceeds any small inconvenience the ministers may have in exercising their ministry. Both parties find that the Eucharist is a common bond that unites them with one another. As the trust level builds, each may find himself or herself confiding in the other, seeking a listening ear or advice. Some find that the other person reminds them of a loved one in their own family, either living or deceased, and the relationship takes on a different dimension than it had in the beginning. The ministry is a mutual one rather than one-sided, where the eucharistic minister is inclined to think that he or she is doing something for the other. The Lord is truly shared, not only in the Bread, but in the exchange of love, concern, caring.

Does this always happen? Not necessarily. Some people are very private and seldom, if ever, confide their affairs to others. Some have been so overwhelmed by life or by their present situation of helplessness or confinement that they are unable to see farther than their own immediate world. This must be acknowledged, accepted and respected by the minister.

### *Qualities Needed in Those Who Minister*

The minister who shares the Eucharist with the homebound will need to be a warm and loving person who has a positive attitude and a happy disposition. He or she must be non-judgmental, friendly but respectful, patient, sincere and accepting of others. It is Christ we carry, Christ we visit, and Christ-in-us who comes to the homebound person. With this in mind, the minister will continually try to develop and nurture these qualities.

### *Learning From Other Ministers*

In beginning their ministry to the homebound, most eucharistic ministers appreciate being able to accompany someone who has had experience in the ministry. If eucharistic ministry is just beginning in the parish, the parish priest may be the one to introduce the parties involved. As the program grows, sheer numbers may make this difficult and a more experienced minister may be the one to initiate a new minister. This not only provides a way to meet some of the homebound parishioners, but it also minimizes the normal apprehension felt by both parties. Once you are comfortable with the procedure, you'll be ready to make the calls on your own.

### *On Your Own*

As time goes on, you will be assigned new homebound persons to visit. You will feel more at ease in making your first call to a new person if you know something about him or her. Although it isn't always possible to have as much information as you might like, there are ways to get some of it prior to your first visit. A phone call to the home to introduce yourself ahead of time and to arrange a time for sharing the Eucharist that is mutually agreeable can provide an opportunity to obtain some information. A few questions can be asked and information shared that will be helpful in putting both parties at ease:

— Introduce yourself and refer to the name of your parish and the pastor so the homebound person or family member will know you are a legitimate representative of the church. People who live alone are especially wary of letting strangers into their home, so the more information you can give them, the more they will feel at ease about your coming. In the case of the elderly or hard of hearing, be sure to speak slowly and clearly enough for them to hear and comprehend what you are saying. Leave your name and phone number so they can reach you if something happens that necessitates a change of plans.

— Ask them how many people will be receiving the Eucharist so you will be sure to have enough hosts. In this way you can often determine whether or not they live alone.

— Asking them how they are feeling, or how things are going for them on that day, will provide them with the opportunity to talk about themselves, thus often giving you information without your asking specific questions. If the information is not shared then, the first two or three visits will usually give you insights into the person and the situation.

### *Rite for Communion — What to Bring*

***Pyx.*** The Eucharist is brought to the homebound in a pyx, a small container with a snug-fitting cover. It is usually provided by the parish church. Eucharistic ministers who wish to do so can purchase one for their use. Parishes that operate with a tight budget might use some of the beautiful pill boxes available today. The important aspect of any container used for hosts is that it have a cover that won't come off easily.

***Rite booklet.*** *Administration of Communion to the Sick by an Extraordinary Minister* is a small booklet that contains the format for distributing Eucharist to the homebound, hospitalized, or residents of nursing homes. It provides several options within the rite. Normally it is provided by the parish.

***Bible or missalette.*** Although the rite booklet contains a few short gospel passages, a Bible or missalette has the gospel reading for the Sunday liturgy. This can be used during the service.

Some eucharistic ministers find it easier to carry a small New Testament with them rather than a large Bible.

*Parish bulletin.* One way of helping the homebound to keep in touch with their parish is through the parish bulletin. Eucharistic ministers can bring a bulletin each Sunday, as well as any other special handouts on a particular Sunday, to each person they visit. Some ministers write their name and phone number on the bulletin especially the first few times they visit.

*Tape recorder.* A portable tape recorder provides the chance for the homebound to hear inspirational music during the service, usually during the time of thanksgiving after receiving the Eucharist. Some parishes tape the homily for the eucharistic minister to play after the gospel reading.

## Explaining the Procedure

When you make your first visit to someone who is homebound, briefly outline the procedure you'll be following. If the person wishes to have a crucifix nearby and a candle burning, by all means respect his or her wishes. This is not required, however. Ask whether the person will be receiving communion in the hand or mouth and whether he or she may need a drink of water to facilitate consuming the host.

In some dioceses, arrangements have been made with local TV stations to air the Mass on Sunday morning. If this is the case and the homebound person has watched the Mass on TV, it isn't necessary to conduct a complete service. A short prayer, the sharing of the Eucharist, a time for thanksgiving and a closing prayer is sufficient.

The time of thanksgiving is an excellent time to introduce taped music that either reflects the scripture for that week or offers hope and consolation for the particular situation of the homebound person. (See Suggested Readings and Tapes, pages 140-142, for suggestions.)

## Pastoral Suggestions

*Fasting.* It is generally recommended that everyone fast from liquids and solid food for an hour before receiving the Eucharist. For those who are — for whatever reason — unable to do so (diabetics, those taking medication with food) this does not apply. Water may be taken at any time prior to communion.

*Spontaneous prayer.* Although the rite booklet is very helpful, it cannot address the need for prayer for the specific needs of each individual. As time goes on and you become more familiar with the person you are visiting, you may want to pray more specifically and spontaneously.

(See Appendix II for ideas for praying spontaneously.)

***Bringing family members.*** Since some homebound persons, especially the elderly, seldom get to see children, eucharistic ministers who have families can inquire as to whether or not they would welcome having the children accompany their parents on some of their visits. Many families today live at a distance from grandparents. Visiting an elderly person is one way for younger children to get to know and appreciate an older person, as well as giving joy to older persons whose own families may be living at a distance.

***Visiting with the homebound.*** Depending on your preference, or the need of the homebound, try to spend some time visiting before or after the service. Sharing conversation is just as important, and just as much an act of Eucharist, as receiving the body of Christ under the form of bread and wine. For eucharistic ministers who have other calls to make, visiting with the homebound after sharing Eucharist may pose a dilemma. Some may feel ill at ease if they still have the Eucharist with them. Others realize that a homebound person may be lonely and they may want to stay, yet have other obligations to fulfill. If you have the time for a short visit, by all means do so. If you don't have time one week, you might try to alternate your visits so that one person can enjoy your company for a longer time one week, another the next week. Another option would be to arrange for a visit outside of the usual communion call or to find time for a phone call.

*Giving and receiving gifts.* As time goes on you may wish to remember the person's birthday or some special occasion. Do this in small ways so they can reciprocate if they wish without going beyond their means. Homemade gifts are especially appreciated and treasured. However, ministers are strongly urged not to accept monetary gifts as "payment" for bringing the Eucharist.

When visiting homebound persons, share as much of yourself with them as you like, but remember to do more listening than talking. Try to be sensitive to their need to talk, especially if they live alone. Take your cues about topics from them. If you know they are terminally ill, are you ready/willing to have them talk about it if they indicate that they wish to do so? Some people are not comfortable visiting a terminally ill or frail elderly person. If this is true for you, it would be best to make known your feelings to the coordinator of the ministry. On the other hand, this might be a good time for someone who is uncomfortable in these situations to ask himself or herself why, and to begin to deal with some of the fears we all have about the future, about aging and death.

### Some Concerns

***Remaining hosts.*** If there are hosts left after your calls, you may consume them unless instructed otherwise.

***Confidentiality.*** As in any service that is person oriented, the greatest requirement in ministry to the homebound is that of confidentiality. The privacy of the homebound person is to be respected at all times. If you receive information that you feel you must share, or become aware of any situation that disturbs you, the pastor or coordinator for eucharistic ministry is the one who should receive the information. Eucharistic ministers sometimes find that they become the confidante of the homebound person even, on rare occasions, listening to what might be considered a confession. (In the early church, Christians actually received forgiveness from one another in this way.) If you sense there is a need for someone to experience the sacrament of forgiveness, encourage that person to speak with the priest the next time he visits, or alert the priest so he will be aware of the need. At times such as this it is important not to ask questions merely to satisfy one's curiosity.

***Emergencies.*** If a homebound person lives alone, you may want to learn the name and phone number of someone to call in the event of an emergency. On occasion, eucharistic ministers find themselves in a situation where, even after arrangements have been made and verified, no one answers the door. Some homebound persons are hard of hearing and a few may be forgetful. Others may have had an emergency arise and may have been taken to the hospital. The minister can check with a neighbor or relative, or a member of the parish staff.

***Requests for other services.*** As each party becomes more familiar with the other, the homebound person may request that other services be performed by the minister. How involved does one become in a situation such as this? If your circumstances allow you to fulfill the request and you wish to do so, then respond accordingly. If not, you can refer the situation to the coordinator or pastor or search out local agencies to meet the specific need.

***Differing backgrounds and values.*** In your role as eucharistic minister, you will meet people of various ethnic origins and/or different value systems. It is important that you respect the individual and his or her values even though you may not agree with them.

***Personality clashes.*** The instances are rare,

but occasionally eucharistic ministers will find that there seems to be a personality clash with someone they visit. They need to ask whether they are to continue with this particular person with the intention of learning and growing from the experience, or if it would be better for both parties to request a change. Rather than seeing this as a failure, it can be viewed as a realistic and healthy choice for all concerned. The homebound person has very few choices he or she can make, and we need not add to feelings of frustration by persisting in trying to establish a relationship. Dying persons in particular have little desire or energy to relate to new people as they prepare for death.

*Conditions in the home.* In the case of an elderly person who may have little outside assistance, it may happen that the condition of the home or apartment may not be what some eucharistic ministers are accustomed to. Unless it poses a threat to someone's health (fire hazard, clutter that could cause a fall, garbage left out for a long period of time) you need to refrain from commenting on the situation. Remember that dust or litter may not be seen by someone whose eyesight is not what it used to be or whose stiffening joints can't bend as often or as freely as they once could. If you think the person would not be offended and you have the time, an offer of assistance then, or at another time, might be appreciated, but be tactful in your offer. Another possibility is to inform homebound persons of any services in their area for which they might be eligible. Some are either unaware of the services, think they can't afford them, or are fearful of letting strangers into their homes.

In one instance, an elderly homebound person was rapidly deteriorating physically. She had no close relatives and the ministers were her only contact with others. Those who visited her became concerned at the change in her appearance over a short period of time. She had always been neat and clean and now it was obvious that she was unable to care for her personal needs or to maintain her small apartment. The ministers tactfully tried to encourage her to see her doctor, but were unsuccessful in their attempts. When they realized that she was in such a weakened condition that she couldn't prepare her meals, they notified the coordinator of eucharistic ministry in their parish. The coordinator called the local Office of the Aging which in turn arranged for a visiting nurse to call on the woman. Ultimately arrangements were made for the woman to be hospitalized. She died not long after in comfortable surroundings and in conditions more in keeping with her dignity as a human being.

One final note: If for any reason you will not be continuing your ministry to certain individuals or will not be seeing them for a while, be sure to let them know and, if possible, tell them why. Strange as it may seem, some may interpret your absence to mean you no longer care for them or that they have done something to offend you. An explanation on your part eliminates any guesswork or unnecessary mental anguish on the part of the homebound.

## Service to the Hospitalized

The eucharistic minister represents the healthy body of Christ bringing care, concern and compassion to his suffering members. It is important, therefore, that the minister take time before exercising this ministry to reflect on his or her mission in a prayerful way. Reading the scriptures that specifically portray the ministry of the healing Christ (See Appendix I) and meditating on the attitude of Christ in each instance, will enlighten and inspire those who undertake this ministry.

### *Qualities Needed in Minister*

How can one determine whether or not he or she is called to minister to the sick? In looking for the qualities needed by those who bring the Eucharist to the hospitalized, the following questions may be of help:

- Do I have a real love and concern for the sick, or does being near a sick person frighten me or fill me with feelings of discomfort or apprehension? Being honest with yourself will help you decide whether or not you're ready to undertake eucharistic ministry in a hospital setting.

- Have I ever experienced illness or undergone surgery and been hospitalized myself? Knowing what goes on in a hospital and having actually experienced a hospitalization oneself can make a difference in understanding what the patient is undergoing. This isn't essential, but it is helpful.

- What is my main motive for wanting to perform this ministry? Wanting to "help those poor sick people" may come more from an attitude of superiority and pity than from a desire to help bear the burden of the suffering Christ. All people have challenges and difficulties at some time in life and appreciate those who are willing to walk with them and help carry the burden of sickness. Our own faith and hope in the healing power of the Eucharist is evidenced by our act of participating in ministry to the hospitalized.

Eucharistic ministers who are just beginning their ministry in the hospital find it helpful to accompany an experienced minister for a few times. Making the "rounds" two or three times with other ministers will show new ministers the various approaches that are possible and help them feel confident in developing their own style within the guidelines provided by the hospital chaplain or the parish of which they are a member.

### *General Guidelines*

The following will apply to almost any hospital situation:

— Always follow the guidelines of the pastoral care department of the hospital where you minister. Knowing, and avoiding, the busy times of bathing and meals will be appreciated by the staff. If you have any questions, concerns or suggestions, address them to the appropriate staff person.

— Since bringing the Eucharist to the hospitalized is a form of hospitality — sharing the eucharistic meal — a great deal is added to the gesture if your manner is warm and pleasant. A smile does wonders and takes so little effort. Try to have each person feel that he or she is the only person who matters at the moment. Be sensitive in your remarks, especially with dying patients. Some may not know they're dying or may be unwilling to talk about it.

— Always identify yourself and give the reason for your visit. If for some reason the patient refuses the Eucharist, make a note of the fact for the chaplain and, after a few words or a prayer, go to the next person. People who are hospitalized, especially for a serious illness, may be dealing with aspects of their past that need reconciling. We need not know the reason for their refusal, and we must not take it as a rejection of us personally.

— If the patient is unable to receive, a brief visit and/or prayer is still appropriate and will usually be welcomed with gratitude. Even these patients can often receive a small portion of the host. Ask the nurse in each instance.

— Some patients in isolation may also be able to receive the Eucharist, since the isolation is often more for their protection than ours. Again, check with the nurse.

— If patients are nauseated, use good judgment about giving them the Eucharist.

Sometimes they will be able to retain a small portion of the host rather than a whole host. If this doesn't appear to be feasible, a short prayer shared with them can be offered instead. Should they vomit the host, gather it up in a clean cloth or Kleenex and wash it down the sacrarium as soon as it is convenient to do so.

— Unless they are seriously ill, sleeping patients can be awakened to receive the Eucharist. A brief conversation or prayer will usually provide time for the patient to come out of sleep.

— Many elderly patients are lonely and may feel abandoned. Try to show that you are aware of this by including it in your prayer. A reference to a similar situation in the life of Christ or Mary can be a source of consolation (Jesus in the Garden or desert, Mary at the foot of the Cross).

— In situations where a patient may be uncovered, one can simply draw up the sheet or blanket before proceeding with the service. If someone is using the commode or a bedpan, offer to come back later or wait outside.

— Confidentiality is just as important in hos-

pital ministry as in ministering to the homebound, and the same guidelines apply.
— Be cautious about getting into any conversation that demeans the hospital, doctor, nurse, or other patients.
— If you promise to pass on a message to the chaplain, be sure to do so.
— The minister is not expected to take on any role of the hospital personnel. Pass on any request for any type of assistance.

*Ongoing Education*

As time goes on, eucharistic ministers will become more familiar with the hospital, its staff and its policies. They may find it helpful to take advantage of as many opportunities as possible for learning more about various illnesses and surgery and the psychological effects these have on the patient. Patients in special units have unique needs: Coronary Care, Critical Care, Intensive Care, Burn Unit, Pulmonary Unit, Pediatrics, Geriatrics, Maternity (Stillborn, Birth Defects), Dialysis, Psychiatric. As one's knowledge grows, so does one's compassion.

## Service to Residents of Nursing Homes

Individual eucharistic ministers who visit a

nursing home and bring the Eucharist provide a service that is very important for members of the parish community who can no longer attend their own church. The ministers come to share the Eucharist with those who may have been daily or weekly communicants in the past and who are now totally dependent on others to bring the Eucharist to them. The ministers are also an important link with the parish community, letting the nursing home residents know that they have not been forgotten. Some of these residents may have been the founders of their local parish and may have made great sacrifices of both their time and finances to build the church and provide for its ongoing needs. They appreciate knowing they are remembered and respected for the part they played as members of the church in the past. Many of them are still vitally aware of, and interested in, their parish and its members.

## *Qualities Needed in Minister*

Along with the same qualities needed by those who visit the homebound, the minister who serves the residents of nursing homes must also enjoy being with older people and appreciate all they have to offer by virtue of their years of wisdom and experience. He or she will need a good listening ear as well as patience with those who are slow moving, hard of hearing or who may not comprehend what is being said as quickly as they once did.

*Factors to Consider*

While more of an effort is being made today to make the surroundings and the atmosphere of a nursing home as cheerful and homelike as possible, of necessity it is still an institution. Schedules have to be kept, thus contributing to an atmosphere of regimentation throughout the day. The minister who brings the Eucharist to residents of a nursing home will need to know the time that is mutually convenient for those involved. Being in contact with the program director of the home helps to keep the lines of communication open.

Most residents of a nursing home share a room with another person and while they may still have a few of their personal belongings from their own home, they have lost any real privacy in their life. Asking if you may enter their space gives them a sense of hospitality. Most will be very happy to welcome you, especially when they realize where you are from and what you are about. However, there may be some who are withdrawn, or on occasion an individual may not want to see anyone or may not feel well enough to have a visitor. Others need time to establish a new relationship and to learn that they can trust you. Respecting this process will often in the long run pay dividends in the form of new friendships.

Try to make the call as personal as possible. In any institution, residents may be known to the staff by their infirmity or their room number. Address them as Mr., Mrs., or Miss unless or until you are invited to use a first name. It is too easy to adopt a patronizing or parenting attitude, especially with the sick or elderly. Using a title adds to the dignity of the persons being visited, a dignity they may feel they lost along with a specific role in life such as wage earner, homemaker, or professional person.

Change is difficult for most people, but especially for the elderly residents of a nursing home. It comes at a time in their life when they are least prepared to cope with it. If you show that you are aware of this, especially during the first few weeks or months, you will offer tremendous support through your understanding and prayer. Knowledge and practice of pastoral skills will be a great help here.

### *Types of Services*

*Liturgy.* In many nursing homes today, the liturgy is celebrated weekly, bimonthly or monthly, depending on the availability of a celebrant. A eucharistic minister who accompanies the celebrant can lead the singing or play taped music as well as distribute the Eucharist to residents who are able to assemble for the liturgy. The minister then helps to bring the Eucharist to bedridden residents who wish to receive. If the number of communicants is great, the minister can use the short form for distributing the Eucharist to those in their rooms.

*Communal service.* On other occasions, the minister may be commissioned to conduct a communion service in a common room or to bring communion to the residents in the various areas where they live. Whenever possible the minister tries to gather together two or more residents who live in one area. This reflects and encourages the communal aspect of the Eucharist. Some residents resist coming together with others for a variety of reasons: They may prefer the individual attention; they may not want to be with a certain person; they may just be out of sorts that day; or they may use this as one opportunity to have some measure of control over their lives.

Try to spend a few minutes with each one. Even if you won't be staying long, sit down near them for the time you are there. This is especially helpful for those who are hard of hearing or whose sight is impaired. In this way, you won't convey a sense of hurry even if your visit has to be short.

In bringing communion to residents in their room, be sensitive to conditions that exist and situations that may arise:

— If the TV is on, suggest that it be turned off or down for the time being. If the resident can't do it, offer to do it for them;

— if you have any doubt as to the mental status of residents, err in their favor rather than deprive them of their Eucharistic Lord;

— if a resident removes the host from his or her mouth, retrieve it in a Kleenex or clean handkerchief and take it to the church sacristy where it can be washed into the sacrarium;

— if you visit some of the people on a regular basis, ask them for their prayers for special intentions for the parish, individual parishioners, for your own family or friends, for the needs of the local community and for the world. Remember to tell them the outcome of their prayers.

## Final Reflection

Visiting residents of a nursing home can be a very rewarding experience. It can also have its bittersweet moments. Most of the residents realize this will be their last "home" before they die. If we can call upon our faith, the faith that tells us that with death life is not ended but only changed, then we can be a source of comfort and support for the residents with whom we share the Eucharist. We may also be surprised to witness the deep faith of those who are ready to surrender their lives into God's hands, not with a sense of hopelessness, but in the spirit of Jesus who said that his life was not taken from him but that he laid it down for those he loved. The witness of those who do likewise will have a profound and lasting effect on those ministers who are privileged to walk these last miles with them.

## Viaticum

Viaticum is a special name for the Eucharist shared with someone who is dying. It is recognized as spiritual food for their final journey from life, through death, to eternal life with God.

It is a unique privilege to pray with the dying. That is not to say that it is an easy ministry. On the contrary, when a minister has established close bonds with someone who is preparing to leave this life for the next, it can be a heartwrenching experience. But for the person of faith there is joy even in the midst of pain.

Ministers who share the Eucharist with the homebound, the hospitalized and residents of nursing homes sometimes have the privilege of being the person who brings the Eucharistic Christ to them for the last time. At this time it isn't necessary or advisable to conduct a long service or say many words. A short prayer, followed by reception of the Eucharist (a small portion of a host if the person is having difficulty swallowing), is sufficient. Sitting quietly by the bedside, occasionally reciting a brief prayer or scripture passage ("Jesus, mercy," "I place all my trust in Thee," "Into your hands I commend my spirit," or one or more lines from Psalm 23) can reassure the dying person that he or she is not alone and that someone cares enough to be present in the final hours.

## Blessings of Ministry

Those who respond to the call to be ministers of the Eucharist are soon in awe of the blessings they receive through their ministry, especially through the people they serve.

Over and above the sense of personal satisfaction they have, the ministers often find themselves inspired by the faith, hope and love of others. These virtues are thereby strengthened and increased in themselves. As one minister phrased it, "I see the Christ I bring emerge in them." New friendships are formed within the community of ministers and with the people with whom the Eucharist is shared. Whereas the ministers may have originally thought that they were giving to others, they soon become aware that they also receive from them.

The final blessing for those who minister the Eucharist is in the form of a promise they believe is to be fulfilled only in the future: "This is the bread come down from heaven . . . anyone who eats this bread will live forever" (Jn 6:58).

With that promise in mind, dedicated eucharistic ministers everywhere continue to serve and to be the body of Christ here on God's earth through their love for others and the witness of their daily lives.

# Appendix I

**Scriptural References to the Eucharist**

Types of the Eucharist in the Old Testament:

> The Passover: Ex 12
>
> Bread and wine of Melchisedek: Gn 14:17-20
>
> Bread from heaven: Ex 16:17-20
>
> Miracle of flour and oil: 1 Kgs 17:7-16

In the New Testament:

> Miracles of the loaves: Mt 14:13-21; 15:32-39; Mk 6:30-44; 8:1-10; Lk 9:10-17; Jn 6:1-15
>
> Institution of the Eucharist: Mt 26:26-29; Mk 14:22-25; Lk 22:14-20; 1 Cor 11:23-27

## Scriptural References to Healing

Jesus heals the sick: Mt 4:23-25; 15:29-31; Lk 4:40-41

Cure of the leper: Mt 8:1-4; Mk 1:40-45; Lk 5:12-16

Cure of a paralytic: Mt 9:1-8; Mk 2:1-12; Lk 5:17-26

Cure of the woman with a hemorrhage: Mt 9:20-22; Mk 5:25-34; Lk 8:43-48

Raising of the daughter of Jairus: Mt 9:18-19, 23-26; Mk 5:21-24, 35-43; Lk 8:40-42, 49-56

Cure of the man with the withered hand: Mt 12:9-14; Mk 3:1-6; Lk 6:6-11

Cures at Gennesaret: Mt 14:34-36; Mk 6:53-56

Healing of the daughter of the Canaanite woman: Mt 15:21-28; Mk 7:24-30

Cure of Simon's mother-in-law: Mt 8:14-15; Mk 1:29-31; Lk 4:38-39

Cure of the blind: Mt 9:27-31; Mk 8:22-26; Lk 18:35-43

Cure of the epileptic demoniac: Mk 9:14-29; Lk 9:37-43

Healing of the crippled woman: Lk 13:10-17

Healing of the dropsical man: Lk 14:1-6

Healing of the centurion's servant: Mt 8:5-13; Lk 7:1-10

Cure of the nobleman's son: Jn 4:43-54

Cure of the sick man at the Pool of Bethesda: Jn 5:1-47

Cure of the man born blind: Jn 9:1-41

Resurrection of Lazarus: Jn 11:1-44

Healing of the deaf man: Mk 7:31-37

Healing of the dumb demoniac: Mt 9:32-34

Healing of the demoniacs: Mk 1:23-28; Lk 4:33-37

Healing of the Gerasene demoniac: Lk 8:26-39

# Appendix II

## PRAYERS

### Divine Praises

> Blessed be God.
>
> Blessed be his holy name.
>
> Blessed be Jesus Christ, true God and true man.
>
> Blessed be the name of Jesus.
>
> Blessed be his most sacred heart.
>
> Blessed be his most precious blood.
>
> Blessed be Jesus in the most holy sacrament of the altar.

Blessed be the great mother of God, Mary most holy.

Blessed be her holy and immaculate conception.

Blessed be her glorious assumption.

Blessed be Saint Joseph, her most chaste spouse.

Blessed be God in his angels and in his saints.

## O Sacred Banquet

How sacred is the banquet in which Christ is consumed,

the memorial of his passion is celebrated anew,

our souls are filled with grace,

and we are given a pledge of the glory which is to come.

You give them bread from heaven,

containing within itself all that is delicious.

Lord Jesus Christ,

who in the wondrous sacrament of the altar

have left us a memorial of your blessed passion,

grant that we may so reverence the sacred
  mysteries of your body and blood,

that we may always experience their saving
  effects within us;

you who live and reign forever and ever.

Amen.

## Invocation of the Holy Spirit

Come, Holy Spirit, fill the hearts of your faithful and kindle in them the fire of your divine love.

When you send forth your Spirit, they are created: And you renew the face of the earth.

O God, on the first pentecost, you instructed the hearts of those who believed in you by the light of the Holy Spirit: under the inspiration of the same Spirit, give us a taste for what is right and true and a continuing sense of his joy-bringing presence and power through Jesus Christ our Lord. Amen.

## The Memorare

Remember, O most gracious Virgin Mary,

that never was it known that anyone who
  fled to your protection,

implored your help, or sought your intercession was left unaided.

Inspired by this confidence, we fly unto you,

O Virgin of virgins, our Mother!

To you we come, before you we stand, sinful and sorrowful.

O Mother of the Word incarnate,

despise not our petitions,

but in your mercy hear and answer us.

Amen.

## Mary's Canticle

My being proclaims the greatness of the Lord,

   my spirit finds joy in God my savior,

For he has looked upon his servant in her lowliness;

   all ages to come shall call me blessed.

God who is mighty has done great things for me,
holy is his name;

His mercy is from age to age on those who fear him.

He has shown might with his arm;

> he has confused the proud in their inmost thoughts.

He has deposed the mighty from their thrones
and raised the lowly to high places.

The hungry he has given every good thing,

> while the rich he has sent empty away.

He has upheld Israel his servant,
ever mindful of his mercy;

Even as he promised our fathers,
promised Abraham and his descendants forever.

## Renewal of Baptismal Vows

Lord Jesus Christ,

you are the king of the whole world.

All that was made was created for you.

Exercise your sovereign rights over me.

I renew my baptismal vows,

renouncing Satan with all his works and his false glamor,

and I promise to live as a good Christian.

In particular, I pledge myself to do all in my power

to make the rights of God and of your Church triumph in the world.

Divine Heart of Jesus,

I offer you whatever I do, however feeble,

to obtain that all human hearts may admit your sacred kingship,

so that the kingdom of your peace will be established

throughout the whole world.

Amen.

## A Prayer of Self-Offering

Lord, I freely yield all my freedom to you.

Take my memory, my intellect and my entire will.

You have given me everything I am or have;

I give it all back to you to stand under your will alone.

Your love and your grace are enough for me;

I shall ask for nothing more.

*Ignatius of Loyola*

## Prayer for Peace

> Lord, make me an instrument of your peace;
> where there is hatred, let me sow love;
> where there is injury, pardon;
> where there is doubt, faith;
> where there is despair, hope;
> where there is darkness, light;
> and where there is sadness, joy.
> O Divine Master, grant that I may not so much seek
> to be consoled as to console,
> to be understood as to understand,
> to be loved as to love.
> For it is in giving that we receive,
> it is in pardoning that we are pardoned,
> it is in dying that we are born to eternal life.

## Psalm Twenty-Three

> The Lord is my shepherd; I shall not want.
> In verdant pastures he gives me repose;

Beside restful waters he leads me;
> he refreshes my soul.

He guides me in right paths
> for his name's sake.

Even though I walk in the dark valley
> I fear no evil; for you are at my side

With your rod and your staff
> that give me courage.

You spread the table before me
> in the sight of my foes;

You anoint my head with oil;
> my cup overflows.

Only goodness and kindness follow me
> all the days of my life;

And I shall dwell in the house of the LORD
> for years to come.

## Prayer Before Sharing the Eucharist

Jesus, you tell us, "I am the bread of Life, the one who comes to me will never hunger, the one who believes in me will never thirst" (Jn 6:35). I come to you with hunger and thirst for this living bread. I believe that in every moment of my daily life, you give me all I need to be another Christ. I thank you for the gift of the Eucharist and for the privilege of being called to share you with others. As I prepare to minister in your name, I confidently pray that I may recognize your presence in every person I meet. May I listen with your heart and speak your words, and may the love you bear for each person be expressed and revealed through me. This I ask in your name. Amen.

## Creating Spontaneous Prayer

Eucharistic ministers who have been able to listen with their hearts will become aware of specific needs of the person they are with. These might be: restoration of health, courage in undergoing tests or surgery, healing of a relationship, need for financial or personal aid, wisdom in making a decision, etc. . . . If there is reason to believe that the person would welcome, or be open to, spontaneous prayer, the minister can suggest it and invite the person to share in the prayer. The prayer you pray with another in a spontaneous way might take place prior to the communion service, as part of the prayer of the faithful, or even after the service if the conversation seems to move in that direction.

One way to offer spontaneous prayer is as follows:

— Take a moment or two to recall God's presence and to be silent in that presence;

— Profess the belief that God knows all things and is aware of our deepest needs;

— Express as simply as possible the need of your brother or sister in Christ, and your trust in God to answer that need. (Refrain from expressing what you think God has to do to answer the prayer);

— Thank God for hearing your prayer and for all his gifts to his people;

— After a moment of silence, invite the other to join you in praying the Our Father or any other prayer you know to be special to the person. Remember to pray slowly enough for the other to be able to pray with you, especially if he or she is seriously ill or has breathing problems;

— If you choose to do so, you can play some taped music to continue the prayer for a few more moments.

# Suggested Readings and Tapes

## CHAPTER 1

*Stages of Faith* by James W. Fowler (Harper & Row, 1981)

*Redemptive Intimacy* by Dick Westley (Twenty-Third Publications, 1981)

*Surprised by the Spirit* by Edward Farrell (Dimension Books, 1973)

## CHAPTER 2

*Experiencing Prayer* by Mark Link (Tabor Publishing, 1984)

*Praying Our Experiences,* by Joseph Schmidt (St. Mary's Press, 1980)

*Centering Prayer* by M. Basil Pennington (Doubleday, 1982)

*How to Read and Pray the Gospels* by Marilyn Norquist (Liguori, 1978)

## CHAPTER 3

*Lay Shepherding* by R. Grantham (Judson Press, 1980)

*Wounded Healer* by Henri J. M. Nouwen (Doubleday, 1979)

*Reaching Out* by Henri J. M. Nouwen (Doubleday, 1975)

*On Death and Dying* by Elisabeth Kubler-Ross (Macmillan, 1969)

## CHAPTER 4

*Growing Old and How to Cope With It* by Alfons Deeken (Ignatius Press, 1986)

*Ministry of Love* by Stephen Doughty (Ave Maria Press, 1986)

*Administration of Communion to the Sick By an Extraordinary Minister*
(Booklet for use in bringing communion to the sick and homebound.)

## MUSIC TAPES

St. Louis Jesuits

Monks of the Weston Priory

John Michael Talbot

The Dameans

## SPOKEN TAPES

"Together By Your Side" by Joseph M. Champlin
    (Ave Maria Press)
    (Aids for comforting those who are dying.)

Other books for lay ministers

| | |
|---|---:|
| **COLLABORATIVE MINISTRY**<br>Skills and Guidelines<br>Laughlan Sofield, ST and<br>Carroll Juliano, SHCJ | $5.95 |
| **QUEST FOR COMMUNITY**<br>Tomorrow's Parish Today<br>Dennis J. Geaney, OSA | $3.95 |
| **CONFIDENT AND COMPETENT**<br>A Challenge for the Lay Church<br>William L. Droel and<br>Gregory F. Augustine Pierce | $3.95 |
| **THE PEOPLE PARISH**<br>A Model of Church Where People Flourish<br>Gerald J. Kleba | $4.95 |
| **MINISTRY OF LOVE**<br>A Handbook for Visiting the Aged<br>Rev. Stephen Doughty | $3.95 |
| **TOGETHER BY YOUR SIDE**<br>A Book for Comforting the Sick and Dying<br>Rev. Joseph M. Champlin | $1.95 |
| **THE PARISH HELP BOOK**<br>A Guide to Social Ministry in the Parish<br>Herbert F. Weber | $3.95 |
| **YOU CAN HELP THE ALCOHOLIC**<br>A Christian Plan for Intervention<br>Rev. Jack Marsh | $2.95 |
| **BLESSINGS FOR GOD'S PEOPLE**<br>A Book of Blessings for All Occasions<br>Rev. Thomas G. Simons | $5.95 |
| **BE WITH ME LORD**<br>Prayers for the Sick<br>Rodney De Martini, SM | $2.95 |

Available from your local religious bookstore or
Ave Maria Press, Notre Dame, IN 46556